PUBLICATIONS OF THE SCOTTISH COUNCIL FOR
RESEARCH IN EDUCATION

XXXIX

LEFT-HANDEDNESS

LATERALITY CHARACTERISTICS AND THEIR
EDUCATIONAL IMPLICATIONS

LEFT-HANDEDNESS

LATERALITY CHARACTERISTICS
AND THEIR
EDUCATIONAL IMPLICATIONS

By

MARGARET M CLARK, MA, Ed B, Ph D

UNIVERSITY OF LONDON PRESS Ltd
WARWICK SQUARE, LONDON, EC4
1957

Printed in Great Britain by
ROBERT CUNNINGHAM AND SONS LTD, ALVA

PREFACE

LACK of knowledge concerning left-handedness springs rather from the multiplicity of studies and contradictory nature of the findings on the various aspects of laterality, than from any insufficiency of material on the subject. The absence of any single authoritative work and the extensiveness of existing material make a more prolonged study necessary for a full appreciation of the problem than the average interested person is willing or able to make.

The present work presenting as it does both an attempt at critical evaluation of previous investigations and an original study of laterality characteristics in a group of normal children will, it is hoped, satisfy a need for a comprehensive report on the subject. The practical problems confronting teachers and parents dealing with left-handed children have been kept in the forefront throughout, in the hope that the information contained therein may make some contribution towards a better understanding of left-handedness and may even lead to a more tolerant attitude towards the 'sinister minority', to which the author herself belongs.

Acknowledgment has been made of all the printed sources consulted. The author wishes to express her gratitude to all those who by their practical assistance, encouragement and invaluable advice have contributed to this study, and especially to her father for his painstaking work in checking calculations and correcting the typescript; to Miss Vida Henning who is responsible for the drawings in Chapter IX; to her colleagues in the Education and Psychology Departments of Glasgow University, and particularly to Professor Nisbet and Professor Pickford; and to the Director of Education for Glasgow and teachers for their co-operation in the practical work.

No words can express adequately the author's indebtedness to Dr Robert R Rusk, Director of the Scottish Council for Research in Education, also formerly in charge of the Department of Education, University of Glasgow. To him she owes any knowledge she possesses of educational research; his was the inspiration which stimulated the undertaking of the present study, and he has given of his time and knowledge to assist with the work from its earliest stages. In dedicating this book to Dr Rusk the author wishes to express her grateful thanks for all his encouragement, criticism and wise counsel over a period of years.

To the Scottish Council for Research in Education for undertaking the publication of this work the author is also indebted.

1956   MARGARET M CLARK

TABLE OF CONTENTS

PART II

AN INVESTIGATION INTO THE LATERALITY
CHARACTERISTICS OF A GROUP OF 330 CHILDREN

LIST OF TABLES

LIST OF FIGURES

INTRODUCTION

ONLY one who has embarked upon an investigation of hand preference can realise the extent of the data available on the subject. No sooner, however, are facts obtained on such matters as the incidence of handedness, its inheritance, eyedness and its connection with handedness, and the effect of these on education, than other research findings are encountered completely at variance with these 'facts'. For this reason it is unwise, if not actually impossible, to state *the* authoritative finding on each aspect without qualification and clarification, and the best way of dealing adequately with the subject appears to be to give an account of the main investigations and offer brief comments on the results. The following chapters are accordingly an attempt to present a summary and critical analysis of at least the more important investigations on laterality preference. The aim has been to present sufficient comment on each of the researches mentioned to enable the reader to follow the argument without having to consult each authority cited. To include as many investigations as possible the remarks are of necessity limited, and to keep the work within reasonable proportions, many studies have had to be omitted, the necessity for this being evident to anyone consulting the bibliography.

Bias is practically inevitable in any study, no matter how scientific it may appear, if not in the actual treatment of the data then in the selection of the aspects to be investigated and in the relative importance to be ascribed to the various results. Apart from being a psychological study, subject to all the vagaries which that involves because of the very nature of the material, the topic under consideration inevitably suffers from a very clear-cut, but nevertheless important, bias. All persons, investigators included, are either left- or right-handed. If left-handed, they are well aware of the difficulties involved in having such a handicap in a right-handed society, and in belonging to a minority group of not more than one-tenth of the population; such appreciation makes their interest in the subject understandable, and makes them in some ways better suited to carry out investigations on laterality than others not so conscious of the difficulties, but they are unlikely to embark on a study which might reveal that left-handedness is an oddity resulting from negativism or faulty training or is a degenerate form of behaviour. The interest of the right-handed in left-handedness is more difficult to understand, probably more varied in its origin, and certainly less direct.

While there are obvious disadvantages in the physician suffering from the disease he is studying, the resultant increase of understanding may be sufficient to outweigh these. It is hoped, and is in fact pleaded by the present investigators that the increased awareness and more intense appreciation of the effects of being left-handed in a right-handed world are sufficient to counterbalance the bias inevitably resulting from membership of the 'sinister minority'.

The first part of this study opens with an analysis of the existing material on left-handedness followed by a survey of the more important theories advanced to explain hand preference. The part played by hereditary factors is discussed in Chapter II. The connection between hand dominance and the development of speech with special emphasis on the studies of the relationship of left-handedness and stuttering is then reviewed. Difficulties encountered in the attempt to measure laterality preferences are next considered, and the relative merits of the more widely used tests of the characteristics are canvassed. The last few chapters are concerned with left-handedness and writing problems, including mirror-writing, and with laterality preferences and reading difficulties.

The laterality characteristics in a normal group of school children, unselected with regard to hand preference, are described in the second part. The type and strength of hand-, foot-, ear-, and eye-preference found in this group are indicated.

This is by no means the first study of the educational implications of left-handedness. It is, however, the first investigation which has studied the various types of hand preference found in a normal population, and is, in character, intensive whereas the others have been extensive. This is its justification, together with the fact that, since the time when the classical studies of the subject were undertaken, the social attitude to left-handedness has been undergoing a gradual change from one of censure combined with fear and distrust to something more akin to faint disapproval. The effect of these changing conditions on the incidence of left-handedness seemed therefore worth studying. With the increased incidence in apparent left-handedness, resulting from the more tolerant attitude towards it, there has nevertheless appeared an increased interest amounting in some instances to concern, on the part of parents whose children are left-handed. Little assurance seems to be gained by visits to teachers or to doctors. Letters in the press and queries on the radio are an indication of both this growing interest in, and concern about, left-handedness. Many of the answers given, however, are misinformed, or express views long disproved, thereby merely perpetuating the negative attitude to left-handedness which has been common to most societies. The results of the study reported here may reassure parents by convincing them that left-handed pupils have learned to read and write without any emotional upset.

The present concern over left-handedness, and the desire for some understanding of its various aspects, shown by parents and others dealing with children, indicate the need for more widespread information on the subject. The publication of the present work may accordingly be justified, presenting, as it does, an attempt at critical evaluation of existing material and a new approach to the subject, which will, it is hoped, be of some interest to those dealing with the left-handed and of some value to the left-handed themselves.

B

PART I
A CRITICAL EVALUATION OF PREVIOUS INVESTIGATIONS ON LATERALITY CHARACTERISTICS

CHAPTER I

THEORIES OF THE CAUSE OF HAND PREFERENCE

THE PROBLEM

IN MANY human activities one hand plays a predominant part. Practice improves the efficiency of the hand used, and so there is an advantage in using one hand or the other. On this basis it might be expected that mankind would be equally divided in its preferences for left or right or that complete uniformity in one habit or the other would be the accepted convention. Instead, there exists a right-handed majority, a general assumption that right-handedness is normal and proper, and a minority of about one in ten which is determinedly left-handed in spite of the difficulties this brings in a right-handed society. This situation provokes speculation and inquiry and leads to a consideration of hereditary and temperamental factors as the cause of left-handedness.

Similar problems arise regarding eyedness and the preferential use of one foot. The study of eyedness has really developed out of investigations of handedness, since dominance of one eye is not so evident to the casual observer, nor does it, superficially at least, appear to present such problems. There are few important actions commonly performed in which one eye only is used, our vision being predominantly binocular, and the fact that in binocular vision one eye is dominant is not apparent on casual observation. The percentages of right- and left-eyedness are not comparable with those of handedness, right-eyedness being about twice as common as left-eyedness.

The preferential use of one foot is more evident in leisure activities involving such actions as hopping and kicking where a trend similar to that in handedness is evident, the larger proportion being right-footed and a smaller number left-footed, though the preference is not so consistent as with handedness.

2

EARLY VIEWS

The existence of a small group of left-handers has been noted by observers from earliest times, references to this being present in the literature of most countries, as, for example, in the Old Testament in Judges XX, verses 15-16, where mention is made of a group of left-handers in the tribe of Benjamin who could sling stones with unusual accuracy. The reference has, in fact, led to the suggestion that present-day left-handers are descended from this tribe. Actually the percentage of left-handers in the Benjamin tribe appears to have been little different from the percentage of left-handers found in more recent investigations. There is no suggestion that the whole tribe was left-handed; the very fact that the left-handedness of certain individuals was stressed indicates its unusual nature.

Though it is not of scientific importance, it is certainly of interest to note the context in which 'left' or 'left-handedness' is mentioned. 'Sinister' and 'gauche' are so frequently used with unpleasant associations that one is inclined to forget that they both mean 'left', while 'dexterity' in the sense of skill is so invariably associated with right-handedness that there is a suggestion that a left-hander will not merely be different but that he will also be awkward or 'gauche'. The evidence that something out of the ordinary, unusual or inexplicable is regarded with suspicion, and even fear, is to be seen throughout the history of man, and the attitude of many to left-handedness is no exception. Left-handedness seems to be associated in the minds of many with something unlucky; in some districts, for example, it was regarded as an ill-omen to encounter a left-handed person when setting off on a journey. Most regions have among their dialect words some term of derision to describe left-handers—'southpaw', 'cack-handed' and 'corrie-fister' being but a few examples.

It was not until the nineteenth century that serious attempts were made to explain left-handedness. The earliest theories were directed rather towards accounting for the right-hand preference of the majority, and tended to dismiss left-handedness as the result of an accident, faulty training or some abnormality in bodily structure. Explaining a right-hand preference is not difficult, but unfortunately the theories which explain this only are inadequate when applied to left-handedness. It is impossible here to do justice to all the theories which have been propounded in explanation of the phenomenon of hand preference, and mention will accordingly be made only of the historically more important.

PRIMITIVE WARFARE THEORY

One attractive explanation offered for right-handedness is the Primitive Warfare Theory, whose upholders have suggested that in primitive warfare man held his stick or sword in his right hand, in order to leave the left free to protect his heart. Thomas Carlyle (1795-1881) is understood to have been the originator of this view when the enforced use of his left hand in later life was necessitated by disease in the right arm. This disability led him to consider the right-hand preference of most men, and to propose that it resulted from the advantage gained by protecting the heart with a shield held in the left hand, the perpetuation of right-handedness resulting partly by transmission of the characteristic and partly by a process of natural selection whereby left-handers became gradually extinct since their form of defence was less efficient.

This theory is of little more than historical interest, objections to it being obvious; the heart is not entirely on the left side; injuries to the liver might prove equally fatal; and, finally, the theory does not explain the sinister minority of left-handers who, so far as we know, still have their hearts in the 'right' place.

THE MECHANICAL AND CENTRE OF GRAVITY THEORIES

These theories are likewise attempts to explain handedness on an anatomical basis. The Mechanical Theory was expounded by Buchanan (1798-1882), a Professor of Physiology in the University of Glasgow, who claimed that immediately a child begins to use his limbs together he becomes aware of a mechanical advantage possessed by the right side. Right hand usage, according to Buchanan, leads to a greater development of the muscles on the right side, but initially this results from the mechanical structure of the human frame. The advantage claimed for the right side arises in part from the position of the centre of gravity of the body. In his first paper in 1862[1] Buchanan dismissed left-handedness as of no consequence, but in his second paper in 1877,[2] he realised this omission and modified his views considerably. He emphasised the importance of the position of the centre of gravity, and suggested that in most people its position is such that it enables them to balance more effectively on the left foot; they accordingly become right-footed, and as a necessary consequence become right-handed. He suggested that left-handedness could be explained by a displacement of the centre of gravity in the opposite direction, while ambidexterity would result when it was so placed that it did not favour either foot. He did not explain how this would occur, nor prove that these differences did actually exist in left-handed and ambidextrous persons.

Though his theory is an inadequate explanation of hand preference, the work of Buchanan is worth consideration, since it represents the views of a nineteenth-century physiologist on the subject. Though part of his theory was the result of experimentation, Buchanan was not guiltless of generalising from one or two instances he happened to observe. This makes it difficult to distinguish what is valid from what is not valid. From a historical point of view it is advisable to take account of these early studies, bearing in mind that much of the discussion contained in them is nevertheless mere speculation with no experimental support, or is based on everyday experience, a notoriously inaccurate source of scientific information.

EYE DOMINANCE

Buchanan's view that footedness explains handedness was followed by a suggestion by Parson that eye dominance is the cause and handedness the effect. This theory was based on the fact that in infancy nearly all voluntary movement depends on vision, and it is according to Parson also the greatest stimulus throughout life. He stated, further, that:

[1] A Buchanan, 'Mechanical Theory of the Predominance of the Right Hand over the Left', *Proceedings of the Philosophical Society of Glasgow*, vol V, 1862, pp 142-167

[2] A Buchanan, 'On the Position of the Centre of Gravity in Man, as Determining the Mechanical Relations of the Two Sides of the Body Towards Each Other', *Proceedings of the Philosophical Society of Glasgow*, vol X, No 2, 1877, pp 390-413

Man has also developed certain dominant single faculties such as speech and memory which cannot be classed as belonging to either side of the body exclusively, but rather to the organism as a whole. In a general way it can be said that we find the neural areas which innervate these highly complex single faculties grouped in the same hemispheres that contain the centres controlling handedness and eyedness. This affords the most direct and speedy co-ordination of sight impressions with intellect, will and action.[1]

In suggesting this connection Parson was anticipating some of the more recent neurological findings on the connection between handedness and brain dominance, but few would agree with him that there is a close connection between handedness and eyedness, far less that eyedness actually accounts for handedness. Two important objections render Parson's theory untenable. First, crossed dominance is extremely common, there being about half as many people who have their dominant hand and eye on opposite sides as there are people with them in accord. Some of these exceptions could be explained away by an enforced change of handedness, as Parson attempted to do, but that would account only for those who are left-eyed and right-handed, while some left-handed persons are right-eyed. Second, it has been found that the incidence of left-handedness is as high among the congenitally blind as it is in the normal population.

Although it is probably not true, as Parson suggested, that all actions are hampered unless the dominant hand and eye are on the same side of the body, there may be actions which are facilitated by this correspondence, actions where hand-eye co-ordination is of particular importance. This is mentioned merely to indicate that though it is generally agreed that handedness does not arise as an effect of eyedness yet it is possible that some of Parson's views about the relation of hand- and eye-dominance may be of importance.

CHANCE FACTORS

In most theories in this group the assumption has been made that right-handedness is normal and that only the small group of left-handers requires explanation. Left-handedness has,

[1] B S Parson, *Lefthandedness—A New Interpretation*, New York: The Macmillan Co, 1924, p 24

then, been explained as resulting from carelessness on the part of the mother or nurse in the way the infant was carried, or from bad training in childhood. Such theories, or, rather, explanations of left-handedness, are accepted by many who completely overlook the fact that left-handedness in many instances persists in spite of all attempts to train in, or enforce, right-handedness, and that it is unlikely, therefore, to be explained by accidental factors.

One cannot omit entirely consideration of such suggested explanations of left-handedness, but since they are far from adequate theories, mention of them will suffice.

EDUCATION

Whereas the former explanations are based on the assumption that right-handedness is normal and left-handedness is abnormal, or at least exceptional, advocates of education as the explanation claim that naturally only a few people are either strongly right- or left-handed and that right-handedness is largely the result of education. This was the view of Wilson,[1] who, being left-handed himself, was not willing to dismiss the characteristic so lightly as others had done. Unfortunately such a theory does not explain why in all societies the swing has always started to the right. It may be true, nevertheless, that only a small number of right-handers are strongly biassed in that direction, and that the preference of the remainder does result from the fact that it is the accepted usage; in other words, many of these might equally well have become left-handed had that been desirable. It seems that one must accept Humphry's nice distinction that the superiority of the right hand is acquired through frequent use, but 'though the superiority is acquired, the tendency to acquire the superiority is natural'.[2]

LEFT-HANDEDNESS AS A FORM OF NEGATIVISM

This theory assumes that right-handedness is the normal well-adjusted type of reaction, while left-handedness is a revolt and completely at variance with the best interests of the indi-

[1] D Wilson, *The Right Hand: Left-handedness*, London: Nature Series, The Macmillan Co, 1891

[2] G M Humphry, *The Human Foot and the Human Hand*, Cambridge, England: The Macmillan Co, 1861, p 202

vidual since society is based on right-handedness. Allowing no physiological basis for left-handedness, and dismissing any suggestion that some hereditary mechanism may be at work in its transmission, it offers a psychological or a psycho-pathological explanation. Burt[1] considered that though some cases might be explained by negativism, others might result from a strong constitutional bias. Blau,[2] on the contrary, maintained that left-handedness reflects a psychological or sociological deviation of the individual. He claimed that there is no innate basis for laterality and that it is developed by training and education and becomes a habitual response by social conditioning. Sinistrality he explained as the result of a deviation in the learning process because of: (a) an inherent deficiency, physical or mental, (b) faulty education, or (c) emotional negativism. In support of this he pointed out that it only occurs in a minority, 'but has relatively greater incidence among males, mental defectives, delinquents, and many psychiatric abnormals'.[3] It seems unwarranted, however, to deduce from abnormals, as Blau has done, the characteristics of normal left-handers.

It seems fairer to consider the possibility, as did Brain,[4] that left-handedness in such abnormal cases may be of quite another type from normal sinistrality. Failure to develop right dominance should not be confused with left dominance though some tests may, nevertheless, lead to such confusion because they class as left-handed all who are not right-handed.

CEREBRAL DOMINANCE AND LEFT-HANDEDNESS

Some investigators suggested a connection between the relationship of the two hemispheres of the brain and the dominance of one hand. At first the belief was held that some anatomical or physiological difference in structure or functioning between the left and right hemispheres resulted in one hemisphere being dominant, and this led, in its turn, to left- or

[1] C Burt, *The Backward Child*, London: University of London Press Ltd, 1937, Chapter X

[2] A Blau, *The Master Hand*, New York: The American Orthopsychiatric Association Inc, 1946   [3] Blau, *op cit* p 93

[4] R Brain, 'Speech and Handedness', *The Lancet*, vol CCXLIX, No 2, 1945, pp 837-841

right-handedness, depending on which hemisphere was the larger, had the better blood supply, or possessed some other characteristic. This implied or assumed that there was some absolute difference which led inevitably to dominance of one side of the brain, a view which is doubted by many neurologists. It is difficult to tell whether an arm becomes longer and more powerful as a result of the use to which it is put or whether the difference in strength explains the fact that it is more often selected for use; it is even more difficult to decide similar questions with regard to differences in brain structure. It was actually suggested by Wilson[1] that the dominant side of the brain is heavier than the non-dominant, and in an attempt to prove this he awaited with some anxiety the death of a person of known left-handedness. Upon examination of this man's brain he found, as he had hoped, that the right side was heavier than the left. Physiologists would now question any such simple explanation. More recent investigators of the subject appear to be much less definite and positive in their pronouncements, and caution is exercised in attributing left-handedness to any one factor, either anatomical or physiological.

Two distinct questions require to be answered to provide a complete explanation of the causation of left-handedness: (1) What is the cause of the right-handedness of the majority? (2) How is hand dominance acquired by each individual? The type of answer to the first question determines to a great extent the answer to the second. If left- or right-handedness is believed to arise from some difference in physiological structure, then genetic factors will be thought to play an important part in its transmission from one generation to the next. If, however, the view is taken that left-handedness results from negativism, or accidental factors, pre- or post-natal, then no further consideration will be required as, on that basis, both questions would be answered, right-handedness being then normal and left-handedness accounted for in each individual in whom it occurs as the result of some factor in his individual development.

[1] Wilson, *op cit*

CHAPTER II

THE INHERITANCE OF LEFT-HANDEDNESS

IN THE nineteenth century, studies of handedness usually tended to be philosophical treatises on the cause and nature of right-handedness. Gradually it became apparent, however, that the stumbling-block in the way of acceptance of these early theories was the existence of left-handedness; such theories as the Centre of Gravity, Mechanical and Primitive Warfare Theories might have explained right-handedness in man, had all men been right-handed. The fruitlessness of these attempts to explain the nature and cause of hand preference led to a change of emphasis. At the beginning of this century psychologists turned to the measurement of handedness, a change which resulted in the accumulation of a large volume of material on single tests, batteries of tests and questionnaires on hand dominance. As a result left-handedness could not be dismissed as an oddity, or attributed to inefficient training. It was felt that though right-handedness might in some instances be no more than the result of training, the same explanation would not suffice for left-handedness which persisted in spite of training. This emphasised the need for a comprehensive explanation of the consistent minority of left-handers, a need which about the turn of the century brought the geneticists into the field.

To assess the importance of the studies of inheritance of handedness it is essential to place them in their historical order, since only then can one ascertain how much information on testing handedness was assumed in each. Some of the theories were evolved at a time when little study had been given to the measurement of native handedness. In some instances the difficulties which might be encountered in any attempt to measure native hand preference were apparently unrealised by the investigator, who selected, quite arbitrarily, some criterion of hand-preference and assumed that this was the only one, or

that other criteria would give similar results, neither of which assumptions was justified. Advances in the measurement of handedness and in the science of genetics in the past fifty years have rendered the early studies of the inheritance of handedness of little more than historical interest. Only if the early naive attitude with regard to the measurement of handedness has been adopted in the more recent studies does it become a matter of some concern. As a preliminary to discussing the various studies of the inheritance of handedness, it may be well to mention the facts to be explained and the difficulties likely to be encountered.

THE FACTS TO BE EXPLAINED

Any theory of the inheritance of handedness has to take account of the fact that one hand is preferred by most human beings for manual tasks and that, while for most people the preferred hand is the right, a small minority exhibit a preference for the left, a preference which persists in spite of the pre-dominance of objects designed to be used with the right hand, and in spite of a deliberate pressure towards conformity by the right-handed majority in society. Though some investigators have suggested the possibility, no convincing evidence has yet been advanced in support of the view that a society has ever existed where left-handedness was the rule and right-handedness the exception. Studies of prehistoric relics and of historical records show that right-handedness has always been preferred by the majority and that a sinister minority has also always existed. The fact that preference for one hand is not evident immediately at birth does not, as some have claimed, rule out the possibility that hereditary factors are operative. There appear to be more left-handed males than females. An impression was created by Buchanan[1] that the reverse was true, but the wording of his paper indicates that this was based on observation in his everyday experience, and has not been sub-stantiated. There may be no hereditary basis for the pre-ponderance found in the studies of left-handed males but a

[1] A Buchanan, 'On the Position of the Centre of Gravity in Man, as Determining the Mechanical Relations of the Two Sides of the Body Towards Each Other'

theory to be adequate should at least take account of their existence. Such a preponderance among males raises the question whether this is an original distribution or whether it is the result of social pressure. In short: Are more males than females born with a tendency to left-handedness, or is it that girls are more ready to bow to convention, while boys are more inclined to be independent or stubborn?

DIFFICULTIES IN EXPLAINING THE FACTS

In addition to all the problems which face any student of human inheritance many difficulties confront the geneticist who takes as his study the inheritance of handedness. The main difficulty is that no matter what test of handedness he uses he will not find all the cases of left-handedness. No society permits the normal functioning of the left hand; on the contrary, all exert some pressure towards conformity, that is, towards right-handedness. If the writing hand were the criterion, in 1860 about 2 per cent would have been classed as left-handed, whereas now it might be 7 per cent or less, depending on the country under consideration. Even were some other criterion used it would still be influenced by the extent to which writing with the left hand was permitted. Different activities are influenced in a varying degree by compulsion to use the right hand for writing, but one cannot doubt that all are influenced to some extent. It is impossible to measure native left-handedness since society's attitude distorts it at an early age, and the actual amount uncovered depends on the test employed. Even the use of a battery of tests does not necessarily produce a completely reliable measure of handedness. This is a problem encountered by all who attempt to investigate left-handedness, and is not peculiar to the geneticist whose difficulties in this connection are further increased by the fact mentioned earlier, that percentages of apparent hand preference vary from generation to generation. Many instances in the parental generation comparable to those in the offspring will in fact not be revealed, even when the same criterion of handedness for both generations is used. The same initial dominance may be led into totally different channels by the different attitude of society at an early stage, while temperamental factors will also have an

effect which will vary with society's attitude, being more significant when the attitude against left-handedness is most severe. The problem for the geneticist is to obtain adequate, satisfactory and comparable data for two or three generations. Some have attempted to adopt the same measure of handedness for each generation using, for example, either a questionnaire on the writing-hand, while others have employed a battery of tests or a single test with the filial generation and a standard questionnaire or series of questions with the parental generation. It should nevertheless be borne in mind that a negative reply to an inquiry about left-handedness in a family is not proof of its absence, but may indicate nothing more than lack of information. If in each generation more and more prospective or native left-handers are permitted to use the left hand this will simplify the task of the geneticist. Unfortunately, as the pressure towards right-handedness varies markedly from community to community, district to district, and even family to family, even within any one generation, one cannot estimate strength of preference from the number of activities for which the left hand is used, or rather, one cannot compare the relative strength of the handedness of two individuals on such a criterion.

These difficulties explain to a great extent the limitations and deficiencies of the studies which have so far been attempted on the inheritance of handedness. Improved methods of testing and of collecting and treating data and the more tolerant attitude shown by society in allowing a freer development of left-handedness, may facilitate a comprehensive study adequate to explain all the facts of the inheritance of handedness.

STUDIES OF THE INHERITANCE OF HANDEDNESS

The earliest studies were those of Jordan in 1911 and 1914 and of Ramaley in 1913. Ramaley claimed that Jordan's first study was of little value as it was prior to the modern genetic type of study, and consisted of selected pedigrees. Ramaley's study of 610 parents and 1,130 children,[1] and Jordan's later study in 1914, of 79 families,[2] led them both to the conclusion

---

[1] F Ramaley, 'Inheritance of Left-handedness', *American Naturalist*, vol XLVII, 1913, p 730

[2] H E Jordan, 'Hereditary Left-handedness with a note on Twinning', *Journal of Genetics*, vol IV, 1914, pp 67-81

that left-handedness is inherited and follows the laws of men-delian inheritance. Ramaley claimed that it is a mendelian recessive probably existing in about one-sixth of the population. The weak point in his argument is that, if this were true, a left-left mating should produce all left-handed children, but as Chamberlain[1] pointed out, Ramaley only cited two families in which both parents were left-handed, and in one of these not all the children were left-handed. Chamberlain adopted as his measure not a questionnaire as used by Jordan (Ramaley did not state his criterion), but the writing-hand, and this resulted in a smaller percentage of left-handers. He agreed with the two earlier investigators in finding that left-handedness was in-herited as shown by the fact that its incidence was considerably greater in those families where one or other of the parents was left-handed than in those where both parents were right-handed. He would not, on the other hand, agree that it was a mendelian recessive.

The most recent study is that by Trankell[2] who has advanced the view that the inheritance of right-handedness can be ac-counted for if it is regarded as a mendelian dominant. He has reviewed the earlier investigations of Ramaley,[3] Chamberlain[4] and Rife[5] and stated that properly treated their results substan-tiated his own position. Trankell's study was carried out on 1,094 children in Stockholm, who were tested by his 'Impulse-Scale', while he ascertained the handedness of the parental generation by a questionnaire. His criticisms of the earlier studies are worth indicating. He claimed that both Ramaley and Chamberlain failed to realise that *individuals lacking the dominant factor might be right-handed as a result of other causes.* He pointed out a further mistake in Chamberlain's data, where a number of families are included in the calculations, families which were drawn from a population different from that under

---

[1] H D Chamberlain, 'The Inheritance of Left-handedness', *Journal of Heredity*, vol XIX, 1928, pp 557-559

[2] A Trankell, *The Genetics of Left-handedness*. Paper read to Thirteenth International Congress of Psychology in Stockholm, 1951 (Based on Chap 11 of *Vänsterhänthet hos Barn i Skolaldern*. Helsinfors: Mercators Tryckeri, 1950)

[3] Ramaley, *op cit*, p 730

[4] Chamberlain, *op cit*, pp 557-559

[5] D C Rife, 'Handedness, with Special Reference to Twins', *Genetics*, vol XXV, 1940, pp 178-186

consideration, in actual fact obtained in answer to a newspaper advertisement, inclusion of which distorted Chamberlain's results. Trankell claims to have proved, and verified from these earlier investigations, that right-handedness is a mendelian dominant; but, as he indicates, investigation is still required to explain what happens in the absence of the dominant factor.

SEX DIFFERENCE IN HANDEDNESS

The evidence at present available indicates that the sex difference in the incidence of hand preference is probably due to environmental rather than to hereditary factors. The variations in the difference found by investigators suggest this possibility. In his 1914 study Jordan pointed out that he now found a greater incidence of left-handedness in males than in females whereas in his earlier studies he had found approximate equality, but admitted that the discrepancy he noted was not sufficient to contradict the general impression that males and females are equally 'susceptible' to left-handedness.[1] Wilson and Jones[2] also noted a sex difference in favour of males, but stated that it was not great enough to be reliable. At the present time there seems no doubt but that there is a greater incidence of left-handedness among boys. In the writer's study of the writing-hand of about six thousand Scottish children between five and twelve years of age it was found that 8 per cent of the boys were actually writing with the left hand, and only 6 per cent of the girls. These findings have been confirmed by other recent studies. No sufficient explanation of the sex difference has, as yet, been presented, but it is at least possible that the difference can be explained otherwise than in genetic terms.

TWINNING AND LEFT-HANDEDNESS

Though there seems to be general agreement that left-handedness is more common among twins than among single born, there still remains a difference of opinion as to whether it is more common in identical than in fraternal twins. It has been suggested by Wilson and Jones[3] that the discrepant results

[1] Jordan, op cit, pp 67-81
[2] P T Wilson and H E Jones, 'Left-handedness in Twins', Genetics, vol XVII, 1932, pp 560-571
[3] Loc cit

c

obtained on this subject may be explained, at least partly, by differences in method of determining handedness or in the criteria adopted and partly by differences in determining identical twins. In their study of 386 twins and 521 single-born Wilson and Jones found a higher incidence of left-handedness in the twins (10·7-12 per cent) than in the single born (6·5 per cent), but found no difference between the two types of twins.

Several hypotheses are proposed by Newman, Freeman and Holzinger[1] in explanation of the excess of left-handedness in twins. They suggest either that twinning and left-handedness are genetically linked, or that the pre-natal life of twins predisposes to left-handedness more than it does to the single born. Though only a very small percentage of left-handers are actually twins, it is possible that the attempts to explain left-handedness in twins may provide some guidance in determining the nature of handedness in general, and for that reason it is worth considering the hypotheses mentioned above. It has been pointed out by Rife[2] that if left-handedness and twinning were genetically linked, then one would expect to find a higher percentage of left-handers among the non-twin members of the families with twins than in families with no twins. This was not borne out in his investigation. The alternative suggestion was that the excess may be explained by the pre-natal life of twins, and, in particular, their crowded intra-uterine position, or by variations in delivery, often found in multiple births. Intra-uterine position is obviously different for twins and affected by the very fact that there are two foetuses. It is worth noting that the excess of left-handedness in twins does not result from pairs of twins being left-handed, as might be expected were there a hereditary basis for the increase; on the contrary, in most cases left-handedness affects only one member of the pair. It was found by Wilson and Jones that between 18 and 20·4 per cent of the twin pairs they examined had one left-handed member. This is supported by Rife who elaborated it further by showing that if one assumes handedness to be a quantitative trait, then the intermediate persons will be capable of being shifted either

[1] H H Newman, F N Freeman and K J Holzinger, *Twins: A Study of Heredity and Environment*, Chicago: The University of Chicago Press, 1937, pp 12, 39-48
[2] Rife, *op cit*, pp 178-186

way by environmental conditions, among which conditions he classed intra-uterine position and crowding; this would account for one twin becoming left-handed while the other is right-handed. Strongly right- or left-handed individuals, on the other hand, would not be capable of being so shifted. Roos[1] investigated whether left-handedness is determined by foetal position. She found no connection between the two, and concluded that some hereditary mechanism must operate to produce left-handedness. Since she did not make a study of foetal position of twins, her conclusion does not necessarily rule out the possibility that the excess of left-handedness in twins may be explained, as Rife suggested, by intermediates becoming left-handed due to the operation of environmental causes. Wilson and Jones pointed out that not only are twins more crowded in the uterus and, therefore, more restricted in their movements but their actual position at birth is also considerably more varied than that of the single born. Their figures are: in 96 per cent of births the head is presented first, while in twins the position is more varied, 31 per cent of individual twins being presented breech first as compared with only 3 per cent of single-born children.

It appears probable from this investigation that genetic factors are not required to explain the excess of left-handedness in twins, and that, in fact, it is more readily and plausibly explained by the difference in environmental factors. If, as suggested here, handedness is a quantitative trait, the intermediates being capable of being shifted by environmental factors, then such an explanation might also account for the isolated instances of left-handedness which appear in some families.

The position may be summed up by saying that genetic studies have revealed that the development of handedness preference has a hereditary basis, in other words, that one's chances of being left-handed are greater if there are instances of left-handedness in the family. Few would deny, however, that factors other than genetic help to determine whether any particular individual will be right- or left-handed, the actual society in which he lives and its attitude to left-handedness, other

[1] M M Roos, 'A Study of Some factors entering into the Determination of Handedness', *Child Development*, vol VI, No 2, 1935, pp 91-97

environmental factors, temperamental differences, and so on, all these play a part in determining whether latent left-handedness will be cultivated or suppressed. These factors will probably have their greatest effect on the intermediates, assuming left-handedness to be a quantitative trait. The environmental variants probably account for the slow progress which has been made in formulating an adequate and satisfactory theory concerning the actual mechanism of inheritance. The increase in apparent left-handedness in the last generation, and also the fact that so many institutions, schools and clinics make a note of the handedness of entrants, should assist geneticists in their attempts to determine the actual hereditary mechanism operative in hand preference.

CHAPTER III

DEVELOPMENTAL ASPECTS OF LATERALITY

EARLY STUDIES OF THE DEVELOPMENT OF HANDEDNESS

STUDIES of the development of handedness in the individual have been carried out by many psychologists in the last hundred years. In some instances these have been directed to providing support for a general theory or particular school of psychology. Watson[1] and his followers, for example, investigated the development of handedness in young children and, as one would expect from behaviourists, favoured the view that handedness is environmentally determined. Others have been concerned with proving its hereditary basis. Some of the studies have consisted merely of observation of the hand behaviour of a single child, either in controlled, or, more often, in uncontrolled situations. Especially in the early work, the observations were frequently made and the report written by a parent or other interested person, a circumstance not conducive to impartiality. The value of the findings of such investigations is limited and they do not afford a sufficient basis for generalisations on the degree of hand preference to be expected with children of different ages. Such generalisations are both unwarranted and dangerous, since the development of dominant handedness is highly individual, the age at which it becomes evident varying considerably in different children, and is in addition affected by various factors not considered in the early studies.

Pioneer attempts to investigate the early phases of hand preference such as, among others, those of Darwin,[2] Hall[3] and Woolley[4] have been followed more recently by controlled ob-

---

[1] J B Watson, *Psychology from the Standpoint of a Behaviourist*, Philadelphia: J B Lippincott Co, 1919, pp 241-242

[2] C Darwin, 'A Biographical Sketch of an Infant', *Mind*, vol II, 1877, pp 285-294

[3] G S Hall, 'Notes on the Study of Infants', *Pedagogical Seminary*, vol I, 1891, pp 127-138

[4] H T Woolley, 'The Development of Right-handedness in a Normal Infant', *Psychological Review*, vol XVII, 1910, p 37

servations designed to determine the stages in the growth of handedness in pre-school children generally.

CONTROLLED STUDIES

Gesell and Ames[1] made a study of the development of handedness and found that in fourteen out of nineteen cases investigated, the tonic neck-reflex[2] was predictive of handedness. In four instances left-handedness was correctly predicted by a predominantly left tonic reflex. They claimed that emphatic constitutional left-handedness is probably correlated with a strong infantile left tonic neck-reflex. Gesell and Ames undertook their study of the development of laterality in an individual in order to find out how soon manifestations of handedness become predictive. They felt this was necessary because of the finding of Giesecke, which they quoted, that there was evidence of transfer of dominance even in the individual developmental history occurring at fairly definite age levels. They agreed with her in finding that certain periods in infancy are characterised by bilaterality or even by considerable use of the non-dominant hand. By the age of two years they found relatively clear-cut right-hand dominance in the majority, and left-hand in most of the others, but at about two and a half years of age there was again a shift to a period of bilaterality. These findings are of importance to those dealing with pre-school children, because they show that predominant but transitory use of the left hand may be found in children under two years of age without necessarily implying left-handedness. It must not accordingly be assumed that because a child uses his left hand on a few occasions he is left-handed. Two factors should be considered: the action in which he used the left hand and the age of the child. Hildreth[3] found that the acts most subject to training—for example, eating with cutlery, throwing and scribbling, show consistently more right-handedness and appear to become stereotyped from persistent usage earlier than

[1] A Gesell and L B Ames, 'The Development of Handedness', *Journal of Genetic Psychology*, vol LXX, 1947, pp 155-175

[2] The tonic neck-reflex is a condition of muscular contraction in which the upper limb is extended and the lower limb is flexed, or vice versa, the head being at the same time turned away from the affected side

[3] G Hildreth, 'Manual Dominance in Nursery School Children', *Journal of Genetic Psychology*, vol LXXII, 1948, pp 29-45

untrained or seldom practised acts. Even in a clinic it is difficult to eliminate the effects of training and imitation; it would appear, however, that these factors do not govern entirely the development of hand preference, although they may retard or accelerate its development.

Generalisations on the development of handedness are nevertheless limited in their application, as there are wide individual variations in the age at which dominant handedness is established, for whereas in some children it is found as early as six or seven months, the behaviour of others up till school age is characterised by alternating use of the right and left hand. There is apparently a close connection between the age at which dominance appears and the degree of dominance; the earlier it appears, the stronger it is, or, according to Halverson, 'the degree of fluctuation varies from one individual to another and is inversely proportionate to the degree of dominancy'.[1] The inference is that to persuade a child to write with his right hand may be more dangerous if the child has shown consistent left preference from an early age, for not only is his dominance probably very strong but it has also been established for a number of years before the interference takes place, whereas if the child does not show definite right or left dominance by four or five years of age, then his dominance, even when established, will probably be less stable. Gesell's results indicated that hand preference may be established earlier in boys than in girls, but he found that in the majority of his subjects right preference had been established by the age of eighteen months, and in 92 per cent by the age of two years. Gesell's studies at Yale Developmental Clinic, with all its up-to-date methods of recording, are probably the most extensive and reliable investigations of handedness in the pre-school child.

Dennis made a study of the early laterality preferences of two non-identical twins reared under a controlled régime from the 36th to the 428th day of life, and confirmed the specific nature of early laterality preferences. He pointed out that many studies have assumed that handedness is a general trait:

It now seems that these explanations are in the embarrassing situa-

---

[1] A Gesell et al, *The First Five Years of Life—A Guide to the Study of the Pre-school Child*, London: Methuen and Co Ltd, nd p 92

tion of having explained 'facts' which do not exist. For there is a wealth of material to show that hand preference is dependent upon the action which is performed and the situation in which it is performed.[1]

As this study was made of twins under a year and a half, and as it was frequency of use rather than precision which was the criterion, this may well have been the more animal type of hand preference and should be differentiated from true human dominance which is characterised by its dependence upon the dominance of the contra-lateral side of the brain and associated with speech development—a subject discussed later in Chapter IV. This suggestion gains support from the finding of Updegraff[2] who made a study, by controlled observation and by test, of a group of two-year-old children, and found that by then definite preference had been established by most of the children, a preference which was the same for all unimanual activities.

Other studies have been made, but one must still adopt a critical attitude to them and remember Halverson's warning: 'The determination of handedness in childhood is at best a very complicated problem', and that 'tests which place a premium on skill or precision of movement rather than on frequency of use or amount of activity may be most revealing for the early detection of handedness.'[3]

DEVELOPMENT OF EYE DOMINANCE

Scheidemann and Robinette[4] sought to discover at what age a child could successfully be tested for eye-dominance. They found that at about twenty-nine months eye preference could be determined by the 'hole in card' method,[5] but that it was apt to be unsuccessful at the first attempts, though they pointed out that the age varies with different children. Castner[6] tested the hand and eye preferences of a group of children, first at three and later at seven years of age, and of the sixteen children tested twelve were consistent in their eye preference on the two tests,

[1] W Dennis, 'Laterality of Function in Early Infancy under Controlled Developmental Conditions', *Child Development*, vol VI, 1935, pp 242-252
[2] R Updegraff, 'Preferential Handedness in Young Children', *Journal of Experimental Education*, 1932, pp 134-139
[3] A Gesell et al, *op cit*, p 93
[4] N V Scheidemann and G E Robinette, 'Testing the Ocular Dominance of Infants', *Psychological Clinic*, vol XXI, 1932, pp 62-63
[5] *Infra*, Chapter VII
[6] Quoted in *The First Five Years of Life*, pp 96-97

while the greatest changes in laterality in the interval occurred in handedness, with a considerable increase in the number of right-handed children and a corresponding decrease in ambi-laterality.

There is thus ample evidence to show that both hand and eye preferences are established in almost all children prior to school age, which discounts the view that the school writing situation is the first indication of right-handedness in the majority, and which negates the opinion that some form of rebellion against school authority is an explanation of left-handedness.

CHAPTER IV

PHYSIOLOGICAL ASPECTS OF DOMINANCE AND THE CONNECTION BETWEEN SPEECH AND HANDEDNESS

In spite of all the investigations on handedness which have been undertaken, our knowledge of the physiological basis of this asymmetry is still limited. Biologists have considered the genetic aspects of left-handedness, psychologists have studied the problem to devise ways of measuring the trait accurately and to ascertain whether left-handers are of lower mentality than right-handers, and educationists have concerned themselves with studying the extent to which left-handedness is an educational handicap. In medicine attention has been paid to handedness, not so much as a subject for investigation and research as merely a trait which should be noted in clinical cases. Mention of handedness in medical or neurological text-books is usually confined to casual references to the handedness of patients referred for brain lesions, where a study is being made of the effect of such lesions on speech. Seldom does a suggestion appear that hand preference is a special feature of behaviour, and that its measurement presents any difficulty. Usually all the information provided is that the patient is right- or left-handed, no indication being given on how the fact was ascertained, how extreme the preference is, or whether it was ever changed.

In general, our knowledge of the physiology of hand preference has been derived from two sources—(1) animal studies in which part of the brain was removed experimentally, to discover the effect on laterality preference; and (2) human studies, obviously confined to cases where brain lesions have been caused by an accident or tumour which have necessitated the surgical removal of a section of the brain. The difficulty in gaining information about the dominant side of the brain arises from the fact that so long as the brain is working normally one cannot ascertain the dominant side, and it is only when the brain is affected by a lesion interfering with speech that it can be known that the affected side was the dominant one.

STUDIES OF LATERALITY IN ANIMALS

Studies of laterality in rats, by Tsai and Maurer,[1] Peterson,[2] Herren and Lindsley[3] and Milesen,[4] have revealed that laterality preference is not a purely human phenomenon. It is only in circumstances where fine manipulation of tools facilitates the development of such skills as carving, and later in writing, that the selection, and consistent training in human beings of one hand only becomes an advantage and an economy in time and energy. The findings on rats, nevertheless, reveal points relevant to the study of the human aspects of the problem, and help to remove certain misconceptions.

The most important findings on 'handedness' in rats are as follows:

1 There is a preferred 'hand'.

2 The majority of the rats studied favoured the right and the minority the left, with a very small number ambidextrous, or rather showing the same tendency to use either.

3 The preference, though fairly consistent within one activity, was normally not consistent from one activity to another—for example, a rat might always prefer the right foot in reaching for food, and yet show left preference in undoing the latch in a puzzle-box.

4 The 'hand' preference of rats could be reversed by destruction of a part, or parts, of the cerebral cortex on the contra-

[1] L S Tsai and S Maurer, 'Right-handedness in White Rats', *Science*, vol LXXII, 1930, pp 436-438

[2] G M Peterson, 'A Preliminary Report on Right- and Left-handedness in the Rat', *Journal of Comparative Psychology*, vol XII, 1931, pp 243-250; 'The Influence of Cerebral Destructions upon the Handedness of the Rat in the Latch Box', *Journal of Comparative Psychology*, vol XXVI, 1938, pp 445-457; 'Changes in Handedness in the Rat by local Application of Acetylcholine to the Cerebral Cortex', *Journal of Comparative and Physiological Psychology*, vol XLII, 1949, pp 404-413.

[3] R Y Herren and D B Lindsley, 'A Note Concerning Cerebral Dominance in the Rat', *Journal of Genetic Psychology*, vol XLVII, 1935, pp 469-472

[4] R Milesen, 'The Effect of Training upon the Handedness Preference of the Rat in an Eating Activity', *Psychological Monographs*, vol XLIX, No. 1, 1937, pp 234-243

lateral side to the preferred hand, or by the administration of a drug,[1] though Kirk's[2] results led him to conclude in favour of equipotentiality of the hemispheres in control of handedness.

From these results the following points emerge:

1 If hand preference is found as low in the evolutionary scale as the rat, then it cannot be dismissed lightly nor explained as being due to chance, social custom or some such factor. If chance alone explained the phenomenon, this would not account for the fact that one rat always reached out for food with, say, its right foot, since reaching is not an activity needing for its performance any fine discrimination, and, accordingly, not one greatly facilitated by the consistent use of one foot. Further, even from the facilitation developed by such a habit a gradual elimination of the alternating use of the right and left might be expected, leading finally to the exclusive use of one to speed up the reaction. This is not found; on the contrary, consistent use of one 'hand' is seen from the first trial. The appearance of 'hand' preference is therefore evidently not something arising solely from environmental factors.

2 Right-'hand' preference found in the majority of rats, as in the majority of humans, disproves some of the early explanations of hand preference, for example, the primitive warfare theory. Ambidexterity, or lack of consistency in the choice of 'hand', appears to be rare in rats as in humans, unless the term is extended to include different 'hand' preference for various activities.

3 In rats, 'hand' preference though consistent within one activity may be different for other activities; this may be compared with the findings on the preferences of young children. Human asymmetrical behaviour, before writing impresses a set pattern and necessitates a degree of skill with one hand which carries over to other activities, may thus bear some resemblance to that of animals. This is true both from an evolutionary standpoint and in the life of an individual. That the evidence does not entitle one to dismiss handedness as of little importance, may be inferred from the following point.

[1] Peterson, *op cit*, 1938, 1949
[2] Quoted in N L Munn, *Handbook of Psychological Research on the Rat*, London: G G Harrap and Co, 1950, p 332

4 Destruction of the cerebral cortex affected 'hand' preference of the rats, as shown by Peterson; this indicates that there must be some physiological basis for the preference and should also serve as a warning against attempts to transfer the handedness of a left-hander. Peterson's results show that long before the development of speech, handedness is connected with one side of the brain.

5 Provided we can generalise from the rat to man, it appears that lateral dominance may be a more localised function of a specific area of the brain than something connected with the whole of one hemisphere. This suggestion, which was made by Jasper and Raney,[1] was based on the finding of Peterson that right-handedness could be changed to left-handedness by a circumscribed lesion in the contra-lateral precentral cortex, and that lesions in other areas did not affect the preference.

Some disagreement remains among investigators, not as to whether there is such a thing as 'hand' preference among the higher animals, but as to whether it is similar in character to that in man. Several writers, including Brain, have suggested as recently as 1945, that in animals left and right preference is fairly equally divided, and that human handedness is closely linked with speech development, and, therefore, quite different in kind. Thus Brain holds that right-handedness is not an explanation of left-brainedness:

Is it not, on the other hand, more probable that it was the appearance of a motor speech 'centre' in the left hemisphere in man that made that the dominant hemisphere, and the right hand the dominant hand, in contrast to the ape, in which right- and left-handedness develop with equal frequency?[2]

Roberts, in this connection, has suggested that:

It is not improbable that the infant passes through an earlier, fleeting, simian phase in the same process of growth by recapitulation. In this phase, rudimentary random handedness may be detected. But true human handedness occurs after the beginnings of speech, by which it is directed and to which it is linked. In the great majority of

[1] H H Jasper and E T Raney, 'The Physiology of Lateral Cerebral Dominance', *Psychological Bulletin*, vol XXXIV, 1937, pp 151-165
[2] R Brain, 'Speech and Handedness'

cases such handedness persists throughout life. Its essential quality is its determination by speech.[1]

Details of the percentages of 'hand' preference in animals are difficult to obtain, since most investigators have studied only very small numbers and percentages deduced from these are likely to be unreliable. Finch (quoted by Brain in support of his contention) tested thirty chimpanzees and found hand preferences in twenty-five of them, left and right preferences being in fairly equal proportions.

One must bear in mind the possibility that human hand preference is preceded by speech development, and possibly determined by it, and that earlier signs of handedness are transitory. This view would gain support from the suggestion of Orton[2] and others that children who begin to speak early, also reveal early very definite and stable hand dominance, not necessarily for the right, whereas late speech development often goes with lack of, or with unstable, hand preference. Speech in man, which has no place in the animal world, may in the process of evolution effect a considerable change in the character of hand dominance. Animal studies though they may reveal some facts which could not otherwise be discovered, have thus only limited application to the problem of human handedness. For information on the other aspects of the subject one must turn to the second source—the clinical studies of patients suffering from brain lesions.

THE DOMINANT HEMISPHERE AND THE PREFERRED HAND

It is generally accepted that voluntary movements of an arm or leg are initiated in a particular area of the contra-lateral side of the brain, and that damage to one side of the brain causes paralysis of the limbs on the opposite side of the body. It is likewise assumed that one side of the brain is dominant in speech functions, and that this is generally the side of the brain contra-lateral to the preferred hand. Like so many general statements, this does not hold universally. Our knowledge as to which side of the brain is controlling speech can be positive

[1] W W Roberts, 'The Interpretation of Some Disorders of Speech', *Journal of Mental Science*, vol XCV, 1949, p 567
[2] S T Orton, *Reading, Writing and Speech Problems in Children*, London: Chapman and Hall Ltd, 1937

only where there is a brain lesion resulting in impairment of speech; in such cases hand preference may be a clue to the site of the lesion. Thus if a right-handed patient has his speech affected by an accident causing a brain lesion, the lesion is found to be in the speech area on the left side of the brain; contrariwise if a left-handed patient's speech is affected, this is accompanied by a lesion in the right side. This relationship was used by the surgeon in ascertaining where the damage was located, and accounts for the references to handedness which are to be found in neurological text-books. The close connection between the centres controlling speech and handedness has been cited by psychologists combating the attempts to enforce a change of handedness; it has also led to the claim that stuttering is caused by changed handedness, a subject which will be discussed in the next chapter.

Most of our knowledge on the areas controlling speech and on their connection with handedness has been derived from pathological cases. This restriction has made it difficult to obtain many cases of the same type, as not more than one patient in ten with an injury to the brain is likely to be left-handed, and not all such patients will have their speech affected; further, in few cases which are the same in other important respects will the lesion be in exactly the same position or of exactly the same magnitude. Recent studies have necessitated a modification of some of the earlier extreme statements on the subject of brain dominance and speech. Two points on which the earlier statements have been modified are: first, the statement that the area controlling speech is *always* on the contra-lateral side to the preferred hand; and second, that the minor hemisphere is useless or completely unused in speech functioning.[1] As Nielson stated:

Chesher has shown that in about 6 per cent of persons, the major hemisphere in language is ipsilateral to the major hand. A lesion of the 'wrong' side then causes aphasia. . . . These cases are encountered

---

[1] E C Chesher, 'Some Observations concerning the Relation of Handedness to the Language Mechanism', *Bulletin of the Neurological Institute of New York*, No IV, 1936, pp 556-562; M E Humphrey, 'Consistency of Hand Usage', *British Journal of Educational Psychology*, vol XXI, 1951, pp 214-225; S Brock, *The Basis of Clinical Neurology*, Baltimore: Williams and Wilkins Co, 1937, p 219

frequently enough so that one should never determine the side of the lesion by the handedness claimed by the patient. In some of these cases a well-meaning mentor has converted a left-handed child to right-handedness at so early an age that the patient was unaware of it. But this does not explain all the cases, because in some of them the patient is right-handed and yet becomes aphasic from a lesion on the right side. . . . *It is impossible to state certainly whether a given person is right- or left-brained until a cerebral lesion with aphasia occurs.*[1]

CHANGED HANDEDNESS AND BRAIN DOMINANCE

Studies have been undertaken not only to find the connection between brain dominance and handedness but also to learn what happens when a child's hand preference is altered. Though many of the statements are mere speculation, some are worth mentioning. Blau stated that:

There is no doubt that after the first few years of infancy the dominant hemisphere takes on a unique construction in comparison to the non-dominant lobe. The dominance trait soon becomes a firmly rooted property. . . . It seems that the dominance decision must be made at about the age of two, a natural maturation boundary line between infancy and the pre-school period.[2]

Many would disagree with Blau's views, since he claimed that preferred laterality is not an inherited trait; nor would he allow that dominance in any form is congenital. Moreover he maintained that the evidence from aphasic patients has shown that 'the neurological counterpart of dominance'[3] remains changeable for several years, and probably even up to early adolescence. The cases where, as a result of injury, the language functions are transferred to the other hemisphere may be instances of the 'minor' hemisphere functioning *of necessity*, because the damage to the other has rendered it incapable of performing its functions, and may not be, as was assumed by Blau, cases of a change of major hemisphere. To illustrate: a person who uses the left hand because his right has been amputated is not, in reality, left-handed in the sense of having a preferred left hand; he has no alternative. It is possibly dangerous to infer from cases of brain injury what is the normal development of dominance. Nielson quotes the case of a boy who acquired left-

---

[1] J M Nielson, *A Textbook of Clinical Neurology*, New York: Paul B Hoeber Inc, 1944, p 278. (Italics inserted by the present writer)
[2] A Blau, *The Master Hand*, p 170
[3] *Loc cit*

handedness, because of the loss of his right arm at the age of ten, which led to a change to right dominance. It appears that the right brain did become completely dominant, though the original major hemisphere was on the left. This was confirmed when, at the age of twenty-eight, he received a blow which brought about a cyst whose site was the right angular gyrus, and the pressure caused aphasia. Thus the left side did not take over the function when the right side was affected, even though it was originally the major side. Nielson stated that there have been cases where left-handed persons have been trained to write with the right hand and have, as a result, developed a writing mechanism on the left side of the brain, but that this usually leaves the right one still capable of functioning.

Roberts seemed to assume that transfer of handedness was only successful when the speech centre was also transferred, and suggested that this was more likely to occur when the change in handedness was close in time to the beginnings of speech. If this is correct, it might explain the instances where attempted change of handedness has been accompanied by retardation in speech development. In these cases either the other hemisphere has not taken over control, or has been slow in doing so, and this would result in at least temporary confusion.

The early investigators seemed to imply that the dominant hemisphere was larger than the other, but it now seems that any difference in the two hemispheres is not strictly anatomical. Some have now swung to the other extreme, and claimed as, for example, did Blau, that any difference between the two hemispheres is a result of the different uses to which they have been put. Such a view does not explain the fact that in some it is the right hemisphere which becomes dominant, while, in others, it is the left. There may be a hereditary basis for the tendency of one side to become dominant rather than the other, but the fact that there is no structural difference makes it possible for the dominance to be transferred from one hemisphere to the other without much difficulty, especially in the early stages. Recovery in cases of aphasia also depends on this ability to transfer the functions of one hemisphere to the other. Nielson pointed out that the enforced use of the minor hemisphere for speech brings about, at first, extremely rapid fatigue, but that

D

patients could be trained to comprehend well enough to get along in life.

The position may be summed up by saying that the dominant hemisphere is generally the controlling one, both with regard to speech and handedness, but that this is not, so far as is known, due to any structural superiority which it possesses over the minor hemisphere; the loss of, or injury to, the major hemisphere does not necessarily result in such permanent and irreparable damage to speech as would occur were there any structural difference to prevent a change-over.

THE FUNCTION OF THE MINOR HEMISPHERE

This aspect of dominance has importance in the study of handedness because the attitude adopted by investigators has coloured their views on handedness generally. Orton presents an extreme example of this, since both his theory of handedness and the principles by which he directed the treatment of his clinical cases were pre-determined by his view on the role of the minor hemisphere. He stated that: 'one side of the brain is all important in the language process and the other side either useless or unused'.[1] While admitting that neither hemisphere is pre-destined at birth for control by any structural superiority, and that if one is damaged the other assumes control, he claimed that most children do have a hereditary tendency to develop the predominant use of either the right or the left hemisphere. Orton's results were based on a study of the development of speech in children, rather than on aphasic patients such as were used in the earlier studies. He did, however, retain the terms used to refer to the effects on functioning caused by brain lesions and apply them to abnormal development in children.

He started with the observed fact that certain children have difficulty in recognising symbols, and in these cases are inclined to confuse them with their mirror-image, for example, mistake 'b' for 'd' or 'on' for 'no'. He observed that some of these children had been changed from left-handedness, while others had not achieved a dominant lead with either hand, and to connect these two observations he propounded his hypothesis that they are to be explained by a confusion between the patterns

[1] Orton, *op cit*, p 27

in the two hemispheres; from this it followed that dominance should be acquired as early as possible if it were not to interfere with the development of speech and later with reading. He accordingly condemned any attempt to change the hand preference of left-handers, as, according to his theory, this would lead to confusion, while it also led him to discourage any attempts to achieve ambidexterity, or anything which might decrease the gap between the dominant and the non-dominant hemispheres. He summed up his views as follows:

The view here presented that many of the delays and defects in development of the language function may arise from a deviation in the process of establishing unilateral brain superiority in individual areas, while taking account of the hereditary facts, brings with it the conviction that such disorders should respond to specific training if we become sufficiently keen in our diagnosis and if we prove ourselves clever enough to devise the proper training methods to meet the needs of each particular case.[1]

For him the method of training included exercises to increase the skill and develop the exclusive use of that hand, right or left, for which the child had the initial preference. This training was used in cases of delayed speech, reading backwardness, and also of stuttering. Though Orton's statements on the reverse patterns in the non-dominant hemisphere have been severely criticised, it is generally agreed that late speaking, for example, is often associated with lack of, or unstable, preference. However, Orton's suggestion that in these cases training of one hand should be undertaken in order to assist the development of unilateral dominance, and his assumption that speech will thereby be aided, have been contradicted by others, who have suggested that he was mistaking a symptom for the cause. According to them the root of the trouble may be late development of the speech nodes and lack of hemispheric dominance, which cause a speech retardation that brings in its wake lack of definite handedness. Brain offered this criticism, and pointed out that cerebral dominance is not itself a function, but is simply a name for the fact that speech and allied functions are located in the same hemisphere. He made an interesting distinction in this connection:

[1] Orton, *op cit*, p 200

The abnormal handedness which so often goes with congenital speech disorders means in my view that incomplete development of speech pathways has left the child without normal hemisphere dominance on either side—a condition incidentally quite different from 'natural' left-handedness.[1]

Roberts also mentioned this when criticising the work of Orton, and further suggested that in these cases 'the absence of speech nodes' deprives the leading hand of the stimulus to real dominance, and indicates that the 'margin of preference' over the other hand must always be small.[2]

It is interesting to note that lack of hand preference can obviously not continue indefinitely, as the school situation necessitates the consistent use of one hand for writing at least, and further that in the absence of a definite and strong preference for the left, the hand used will be the right. It is well to remember that *use of the right hand does not necessarily mean choice of the right*; on the contrary, it merely indicates absence of determination to use the left. In the cases where use of the right hand is merely indicative of absence of a preference for either, it is probable that the 'margin of preference', as indicated by Roberts, is small; but we must await further research before we can say what is the exact effect of such a condition on the learning capacity, though it does appear that the children in the group stressed by Orton, that is, those lacking in definite dominance, or as he called them the 'Motor Intergrades', may have characteristic learning troubles.

AMBIDEXTERITY AND RETARDED SPEECH

In ambidextrous patients the effects of a brain lesion on speech are more difficult to predict, though, in general, a unilateral lesion does not cause severe aphasia. In some cases, however, it has been found that a lesion in either hemisphere may cause damage, but that it may not be so severe or so lasting as would be expected from the site of the lesion. These are possibly, according to Nielson, cases of sinistrality for some functions and dextrality for others.

Mention has already been made of Orton's finding that delayed speech appears to be associated with lack of early development of dominant handedness. Some investigators have

[1] Brain, *op cit*, p 841   [2] Roberts, *op cit*, p 570

claimed that there is no such thing as true ambidexterity, and that the people we are inclined to call ambidextrous are merely instances of changed left-handers. Gesell[1] claimed that asymmetrical behaviour is the normal human mode of adjustment, and that symmetrical or ambidextrous behaviour would be abnormal. There are, however, instances where lack of hand preference has been accompanied by lack of development in other respects, notably in speech. In describing these cases, Galen (quoted by Orton) coined the word 'ambilevous', to imply having two left hands, to exclude the idea of skill connoted by the term 'ambidextrous'.

Several investigators claimed to find a higher incidence of left-handedness among mental defectives than in the normal population. Brain and Roberts suggested that there might be two types of left-handedness, namely, normal dominance of the left hand and the right brain, similar to right-hand dominance, and an inferior type, in which the dominance is less stable and both hands unskilful. In certain classifications representatives of the second type would be regarded as left-handed, since they would use their left hand for some activities. Brain suggested that these cases might explain the higher incidence of supposed left-handedness found in some abnormal groups, for example, among mental defectives. Roberts pointed out that this type of handedness will be found especially in speechless defectives, since handedness will not there be under the control of speech, which he considered necessary to its normal development. It would appear, therefore, that Galen's ambilevous group, Brain's second type of left-handers where the preference is unstable, and even some of Orton's cases of developmental apraxia, or abnormal clumsiness, have much in common. The most fruitful line for further research on this aspect of indecisive handedness, or what some would call a form of ambidexterity, would appear to be in the neurological field by electro-encephalographic studies. No difference in the electro-encephalographic records of right- and left-handed persons have been found characteristic of the two types of dominance, but, as was mentioned earlier, there have been cases

[1] *Manual of Child Psychology*, ed L Carmichael, New York: John Wiley and Sons Inc, 1946, p 307

where abnormal clumsiness was connected with a brain lesion which was revealed by the electro-encephalographic tracing. It is now necessary to learn how frequently that type of case is present in the normal population, and whether many of the cases of delayed speech, or lack of development of skill with either hand, or a combination of both are, in fact, due to some organic deficiency or developmental disorder which has eluded the earlier investigators, to whom delicate instruments for diagnosis were not available. With the introduction of the electro-encephalograph it may no longer be necessary to await a lesion resulting in aphasia before acquiring knowledge of the working of the brain; as new techniques for using the apparatus are devised discoveries may be made concerning the normal working of the brain, as far-reaching in their effects as the early results of Jackson and Head from pathological cases.

These neurological findings show that there is at least an intimate connection between the development of speech and dominant handedness, and suggest that there may be some connection between retarded speech and lack of dominance. The next chapter will be devoted to a study of stuttering and handedness which, though actually only one aspect of the subject of speech and handedness, is yet of sufficient practical importance to warrant special consideration. In addition, it is a topic which has been the centre of considerable controversy and for that reason it seems necessary to cite at least the more important investigations and to indicate the facts which have been established.

CHAPTER V

STUTTERING AND HANDEDNESS

THE relationship between left-handedness and stuttering has possibly more practical importance than any other aspect of the problem of handedness. Certainly, the suggestion that there might be some connection between these two conditions has led to a considerable volume of research with the specific aim of proving or disproving a direct association between changed handedness and stuttering. The first studies in which this possibility was revealed seemed to achieve widespread publicity, and were generally regarded as findings of serious import. The impression was created, as a result, that if a child who showed left-handed tendencies were forced to use his right hand, stuttering would *automatically* follow.

This early view induced a fear in many parents and teachers, resulting in a 'hands-off' policy in connection with left-handedness, a fear which lasted for a number of years. This period was characterised by a more tolerant, or perhaps it would be more accurate to say, a more cautious attitude to left-handers, and during it they were allowed, though with half-suspicious contempt, to use the left hand. It was pointed out at frequent intervals, however, both to them and to others, that actions performed with the left hand are considerably inferior and more awkward than those carried out with the 'proper' hand—the right. This attitude to left-handers has widely persisted to the present day, and it is still very common to hear both teachers and parents express opinions on left-handedness which reflect these partly unconscious sentiments. Within the last few years evidence has been forthcoming that the connection between changed left-handedness and stuttering is not absolute as was at first believed, and, with this reassurance, those in authority have tended to return to their earlier policy of insistence on right-hand training. They base their altered conduct on evidence which they claim reveals that actions performed with the left hand are less efficient than those with the right, and that it is consequently better for everyone concerned if all use the right hand. Their second justification for changing left-handers is that research has shown, they claim, that changed handedness has no effect on speech, and for further support they cite instances of people of their personal acquaintance who have been changed to the right hand for writing and have suffered no visible ill-effects. It is probably true to say that this is a fairly accurate picture of the general attitude adopted to-day by many people in most countries. Some left-handers are permitted to write with the left hand, but by no means all; while few people realise just how common it still is for left-handers to be encouraged or forced to use their right hand. Frequently the change is carried out before the child enters school; but even when it takes place later, in this country at least, the change is still usually made by the parents rather than the school, though the same is not true of continental countries. The controversial subject of whether to change a left-handed child and make him use his right hand will be treated more fully in a later chapter. We are concerned here more directly with a consideration of the more general aspects of stuttering, a survey of the researches which have been carried out on the connection between stuttering and handedness, and a critical analysis of the significance of these for the problem of handedness.

STUTTERING

Stuttering may result either from physiological or psychological causes. Though there is possibly no exact line of demarcation between the two types, there are at one extreme cases where there is evidently a physiological etiology and at the other extreme cases where no such cause can be discovered and where the origin of the trouble is mainly psychological. McAllister[1] discusses in some detail a selection of cases where the stuttering was directly attributable to an organic defect caused, for example, either by defective conditions of the nasal passages, or by defective functioning of the respiratory muscles. There

[1] A H McAllister, *Clinical Studies in Speech Therapy*, London: University of London Press, 1937

are no speech organs as such. Speech is carried out only on the expiration of breath, and necessitates for its correct production a steady even flow of breath, which means that jerkiness in the breath, from any cause, will be reflected in speech. These two facts mean that any disease of the nasal passages or of the respiratory muscles may cause that form of interrupted speech known as stuttering. Where such physiological factors are present any emotional concomitant shown by the stutterer has probably been caused by the actual stuttering, resulting from the attitude of others to the abnormality. Such clear-cut instances are, however, seldom encountered, most cases having at least some psychological elements in their etiology. It is with this type that we are more concerned here.

Many speech therapists have held that behaviour which we are inclined to regard as part of the make-up of stutterers is not actually present in the early stages of stuttering, but develops gradually, increasing each time the stutterer attempts unsuccessfully to make himself understood. The embarrassment, fear of speaking, shunning of company, and many introvertive characteristics which we see in the adult stutterer are, on this view, defences built up by the stutterer resulting from the stuttering. These tendencies are not innate in the stutterer, nor are attempts on his part to avoid situations in which the disability will be evident. They are increased when the stutterer has been teased or subjected to ridicule because of his abnormality, but they appear to develop even where no actual references have been made to the speech difficulty. A tendency to avoid the stutterer, and often on the part of the teacher a tendency to avoid asking him to read or answer questions, though this in most instances is done out of sympathy or consideration for his feelings, may accentuate the stutterer's diffidence, since he cannot remain unaware of all the subtle differences in treatment to which he is subjected. The evidence in support of this suggestion, that the emotional reactions associated with stuttering result from the defect, is verified by examination of child stutterers in the very early stages of stuttering, when it is found that the emotional content is slight or lacking, and by the statements of cured adult stutterers who frequently admit their previous fear of speaking and their avoidance of situations where they might be required to speak. Questioning of these cured stutterers reveals the numerous defences to which they resort in attempts to prevent the worst of the stuttering from being noticed. These interesting aspects of the subject have been dealt with at great length by Van Riper[1] who was himself a cured stutterer. Part of his treatment was directed to forcing the patients into situations which they had previously shunned, and where they would require to speak, but supporting them in advance with as many devices as possible for dealing at a conscious level with the difficulties they would meet in these situations. Van Riper and others have found that when the stutterer was cured and knew that he had nothing to fear from his speech and that he would no longer have to face the likelihood of appearing odd in the company of others, his personality underwent an apparently astonishing change. He was no longer a shy, inhibited introvert, since he had now the ability to enjoy social communication. It is a well-known fact that a number of great orators had some speech difficulty which they overcame, and having mastered their handicap they used speech both as a means of social communication and of commanding power.

The connection between emotional factors and stuttering requires to be indicated as a preliminary to the consideration of changed handedness and speech. If stuttering results from a motor disturbance, as many have suggested, then the probability of changed handedness being a causative factor in stuttering is greatly reduced. Kopp[2] insisted that more emphasis should be placed on the connection between stuttering and motor disturbances, and she stated that gross hereditary defects of the motor function and disturbances of various motor systems are usually found in stutterers. Bryngelson[3] pointed out that the interruptions of speech in the early stages of stuttering are short and tensionless and that at these early stages the spasms resemble unobtrusive interruptions of the breath stream and only later become a specific handicap to communication as a

[1] C Van Riper, *Speech Correction, Principles and Methods*, New York: Prentice-Hall Inc, 1947

[2] H Kopp, 'The Relationship of Stuttering to Motor Disturbances', *Nervous Child*, vol II, No 2, 1942, pp 107-116

[3] B Bryngelson, 'Stuttering and Personality Development', *Nervous Child*, vol II, No 2, 1942, pp 162-166

result of the psychological factors. He maintained, however, that there is no motor trouble known in medicine where no deviation from normal speed takes place. From the variety of views expressed on this subject it would appear that one's decision on the chief contributory causes of stuttering is affected by one's attitude to other aspects of behaviour, and that some factor other than the actual stuttering is decisive in determining these views.

This is not the place for a detailed discussion of all aspects of stuttering, its causes and special features. There are, however, a number of points which seem to be universally accepted and which have relevance for this study.

1 All investigators agree that *stuttering is a malady of child-hood*, being specially prone to commence between the ages of three and five years. Hildreth[1] stated that 85 per cent of cases show the trait before the age of six, and rarely after nine years of age; Bryngelson's[2] figures were 90 per cent before seven years of age. It has been stated by West[3] that even in the few cases where stuttering is not noticed until adult life, it may have occurred earlier but been so slight that it did not attract attention, or the conditions of the social environment may have been so favourable at the early stage that its onset was delayed. Thus, though the period of learning to speak is comparatively short, it is of great importance, and it is at this stage more than at any other that disturbances of an emotional kind are most likely to be detrimental to normal speech development.

2 There appears to be a connection between late development of speech and stuttering, though it has often been pointed out that stuttering is found even in those of high intelligence.

3 The incidence of stuttering is very much higher among boys than among girls. West stated that the ratio varies from 8·1 to 3·1, depending on the respective ages, and that very few female adults stutter.

4 According to Hildreth stuttering is only found in civilised

---

[1] G Hildreth, 'Development and Training of Hand Dominance: IV, Developmental Problems Associated with Handedness', *Journal of Genetic Psychology*, vol LXXVI, 1950, pp 39-100
[2] Bryngelson, *op cit*, pp 162-166
[3] R West, 'The Pathology of Stuttering', *Nervous Child*, vol II, No 2, 1942, pp 97-106

races where reading and writing are taught, and where there is rigid training in social manners involving manual acts. It was pointed out by Chrysanthis[1] that racial factors affect stuttering, and that stuttering is unknown among the Chinese. He carried out an investigation of stuttering among Greek school children and found that there was a higher incidence amongst them than among children of other European countries. The percentages he quoted were: Greece 1·85, Belgium 1·4, Hungary 1·02, Sweden 1·8 and the United States 0·87.

5 Stuttering is not evenly distributed throughout the population, its incidence being greater in certain families than in others. In other words, it is likely that among the relatives of the stutterer will be found others who also have a stutter, and this cannot be explained by imitation, since frequently the stuttering members have no contact with one another. It appears, in any case, that stuttering is seldom caused by imitation, and even if it is, there must be present in the imitator some weakness which makes him prone to stutter; further, it is often found, on examination of these supposed imitators, that the nature of the stutter is quite different from the form 'imitated'. It would be incorrect to say that stuttering is inherited; but it may be somewhat similar to tuberculosis, in the sense that, though the disease is not inherited the tendency to acquire it may be, and that given certain conditions some individuals will develop a stutter while others will not. Not much information on organic differences between stutterers and non-stutterers exists, but it has been claimed by West that there is a difference in metabolic rate and that there is a slowness in repetitive movements in stutterers, particularly those movements involved in speech; also, that stutterers have a tendency to certain diseases of the respiratory tract. Hildreth claimed that stutterers show a marked disturbance of motor function.

6 It has been maintained by West[2] that in families where there is a high incidence of stuttering there is also more than the expected amount of twinning. Macmeeken[3] claimed that there is also a higher incidence of left-handedness in families

[1] K Chrysanthis, 'Stammering and Handedness', *Lancet*, vol CCLII, 1947, pp 270-271   [2] West, *op cit*
[3] A M Macmeeken, *Developmental Aphasia in Educationally Retarded Children*, London: University of London Press, 1942

where twinning and stuttering appear, suggesting some connection between the three conditions.

HANDEDNESS AND STUTTERING

These six findings on stuttering have been quoted because they have all some bearing on the relation between handedness and speech. The first three may be considered together—that stuttering usually appears before the age of six years, that it may be associated with delayed speech and that it is commoner in boys than in girls. McCarthy in a chapter on the 'Language Development in Children' directed attention to the fact that 'most studies report a higher incidence of left-handedness and a higher incidence of stuttering and also of reading disabilities among boys, who in comparison with girls are slightly more retarded in all measures of linguistic development'. She also suggested that there may be a relation between linguistic development and motor development, 'and more specifically between linguistic development and the establishment of lateral dominance'.[1] A direct connection between them has not been definitely established, but from studies of quite different aspects of the problem the same suggestion has also been advanced by others, notably Brain[2] and Orton.[3] In support of the possibility of a direct connection between speech development and lateral dominance there may be adduced: first, that both are the concern of the same side of the cerebral hemisphere; and second, that the development runs parallel in time. It has been claimed that late speech development has often been evident in stutterers and further that there is a connection between handedness and retarded speech; but whether we are justified in concluding that the third connection is present, namely, that between left-handedness and stuttering, is another matter.

The other three points mentioned earlier, namely, that the incidence of stuttering varies from country to country, that more stuttering is found in certain families than in others, and that in these families there is frequently a high incidence of twinning, have an even more direct connection with handedness. There

---

[1] *Manual of Child Psychology*, ed L Carmichael, p 546
[2] R Brain, 'Speech and Handedness'
[3] S T Orton, *Reading, Writing and Speech Problems in Children*

are probably many ways of explaining the variation in the incidence of stuttering in different countries. It is possible that certain languages are more complicated to learn than others, and that the incidence of stuttering may be in some way connected with language difficulty. It is, however, at least probable that the countries where the amount of stuttering is higher than normal may also be countries where a more rigid conformity to certain standards of manual behaviour is required. It may not be the actual standard of conformity which is the direct cause of the increase, but something more subtle. Perhaps the emotional consequences and the stress resulting from this insistence may precipitate stuttering in cases where, given favourable conditions, it might not have occurred. The fact that one country where the percentage of stuttering is low is the United States, makes the suggestion feasible, since that is one of the countries which largely permitted children to use the preferred hand for manual tasks, including writing, whereas the incidence of stuttering is higher, for example, in Sweden and Germany where right-hand usage is adhered to more strictly. It should be made clear that this suggestion does not imply that changed handedness is the cause of stuttering, but merely that it is a possible explanation of the greater incidence in certain countries, since the changed handedness in these countries might result in stuttering in some marginal cases where there would otherwise have been none; in these cases it may have acted as a precipitating, rather than a causal, factor.

In families where the incidence of stuttering is high, the incidence of left-handedness is likewise high and though this does not necessarily mean that all stutterers are left-handed or that all left-handers stutter, it does imply a greater possibility of stutterers being left-handed than if both 'abnormalities' were randomly distributed throughout the population. The danger is in drawing the unwarranted conclusion that there will be a large number of stutterers who are left-handed. In short, even were the percentage of stutterers four times as great among left-handers as it actually is in the normal population this would not entitle us to consider left-handedness a major cause of stuttering. This misconception has had much to do with fostering the idea that changed handedness causes stuttering, and many in their attempts to disprove it have concentrated on the wrong aspect of the problem. It appears that the contradictory findings on this subject are to some extent attributable to a confusion between the two issues: firstly, that forced changed handedness may result in stuttering; and secondly, that stuttering is caused by changed handedness. The second suggestion does not, as some have assumed, follow from the first.

CHANGED HANDEDNESS AND STUTTERING

The strongest advocates of the view that there is a causal connection between stuttering and left-handedness, or stuttering and lack of dominance caused by attempts to change hand preference, have been Travis, Orton and Van Riper. Travis stated that failure to develop dominance, and interference with the development of a dominant physiologic lead are very closely related to stuttering. In support of this view he quoted, first, the finding of Bryngelson who reported that of his 200 stutterers, 62 per cent were originally left-handed and had been required to change to the right; and second, that 'in the University of Iowa Speech Clinic, of the several hundred right-handed stutterers who have been examined within the past three years 43 per cent were originally left-handed'.[1]

Orton, like Travis, emphasised the necessity for creating a dominant hemisphere, and claimed, as was mentioned earlier, that delay in acquiring this dominant lead would retard speech development. It would, according to Orton, also tend to induce stuttering. He differentiated stutterers into two types: those who have some speech impediment from the time they first begin to talk, that is, from about two or three years of age; and secondly those who speak normally until about the age of six or eight years, at which stage stuttering occurs. Thus he claimed that there are two critical periods in the development of speech, and that in the instances where a speech impediment, such as stuttering, develops at the early stage it is associated with some delay in beginning to speak and in the development of preferential handedness. The second critical period occurs about the time when the child is learning to read and write, and

[1] L E Travis, *Speech Pathology*, New York: D Appleton-Century Co, 1931, pp 139-140

he claimed that children who develop a stutter at that stage often also have a writing disability. Orton divided childhood stutterers into four categories: (a) where an enforced shift of handedness was carried out by the parent or nurse; (b) where the child has been slow in acquiring a preference for one particular hand, or, in his words, showed 'motor intergrading'; (c) where there was no evidence of handedness shift, but a very strong family history of stuttering; (d) where there was no change of handedness, no evidence of intergrading and no other case of stuttering in the family. In connection with this last group, however, Orton claimed that 'in the majority of instances of these sporadic cases, disorders of the language faculty of other types or the presence of a familial tendency toward left-handedness can be found by proper inquiry'.[1] He laid great stress on his first two categories mentioned above, and emphasised the importance of 'motor intergrading' in stuttering and other language disorders.

Van Riper[2] also, when treating stutterers, considered that a history of any tendency towards left-handedness was of particular importance. He claimed that stutterers performed more like ambidextrous subjects than like normal right- or left-handers when tested on his Critical Angle Board.[3] This claim would support Orton's suggestion that the hand preference of stutterers is not so firmly established as that of normal people (his motor intergrades). Van Riper's finding, however, has since been criticised by Johnson and King,[4] who claim that his supposed ambidextrous subjects were, in fact, actually representative of the normal population, while his right- and left-handed cases were extremes, thus implying that all he had in reality proved was that the stutterers' performance was not in essentials any different from that of the normal population. Van Riper[5] emphasised the importance of changed handedness in

[1] Orton, op cit, p 125
[2] C Van Riper, 'The Quantitative Measurement of Laterality', Journal of Experimental Psychology, vol XVIII, 1935, pp 372-382
[3] Infra, Chapter VI for details of the test
[4] W Johnson and A King, 'An Angle Board and Hand Usage Study of Stutterers and Non-Stutterers', Journal of Experimental Psychology, vol XXXI, 1942, pp 293-311
[5] C Van Riper, Speech Correction, Principles and Methods

connection with stuttering, and drew attention to the difficulty of obtaining reliable histories of changed handedness because of the time which had usually elapsed since the change, and because also of the reluctance of parents to admit that such an action on their part might have been a causal factor in the stuttering.

Both Travis and Orton, like West, regarded stuttering from the neurological angle; the bias of other workers is towards the emotional, even though they place a similar emphasis on the importance of changed handedness.

The treatment prescribed for stutterers by Travis, Orton and Van Riper was greatly influenced by their insistence on the importance of changed handedness or lack of dominance, and they often prescribed, as a major part of their treatment of stutterers, a return to the preferred hand. Orton prescribed that this should only be attempted if the previously preferred hand had acquired sufficient motor ability. His emphasis on lack of dominance as a cause of stuttering led him to suggest that in such cases measures should be used to promote the lead of the master hand, and thereby increase the gap between the dominant and non-dominant hemispheres. He did state, nevertheless, that where there had been an enforced change of handedness, 'retraining of all unilateral activities in the native hand is always worth the experiment and is often accompanied by a fairly prompt cessation of the stuttering'.[1] The general impression likely to be derived from a study of the works of Travis, Orton, Van Riper and other writers of the same school of thought is that miraculous cures of stuttering are to be expected simply from a retraining of the left hand, if not in all cases, then certainly in some. Orton did point out that to cite instances where a change of handedness has cured the stuttering does give the impression that all stutterers might have been left-handed and should be retrained:

This rests on a very superficial comprehension of the complexities of the problem of cerebral dominance and of the potential sources of difficulty. In many cases there is no superiority of the left hand and no indication of an enforced change from the native pattern. Many of them are marked motor intergrades with no clear preference for either hand, but some—and this applies particularly to those with a very

[1] Orton, *op cit*, p 194

strong hereditary lading towards stuttering—are as clearly as we can determine exclusively right-sided from the beginning.[1]

Such a warning has not been sufficient to prevent the wrong impression being gained from a study of the rest of the book— and from other books in a similar vein—that stuttering was *apparently* cured by nothing more than a change of handedness. 'Apparently' is emphasised in this connection since no treatment at a clinic would in reality consist solely of training handedness. The very fact of attending the clinic has often some psychological importance, and frequently the effect is greatest on the parent, where it is most required, whose attitude may be incidentally as much changed to the stuttering as to the hand preference. Probably the greatest danger has arisen, not so much from the original writers, but rather from the use of their examples by others, who in removing them from their context have given them an undue significance.

Johnson and Duke[2] made a study of sixteen cases where changed handedness was associated with stuttering, and considered its importance in connection with the onset of stuttering and also with its disappearance. The value of their investigation results in part from the reasoned way in which they interpreted the findings, and in part from the fact that they made no extravagant claims. They pointed out that in certain cases where an enforced change of handedness had been found along with stuttering, the stuttering was cured without any return to the preferred hand. Further, they drew attention to an important fact, which is often ignored, that where the reversion to the preferred hand was undertaken in the belief that this would in some way benefit speech, the significance of the suggestion could not be estimated but should not be overlooked. They pointed out that in none of the cases investigated by them could all other etiological factors be ruled out; in other words, in all cases where there was a change of handedness there was also some other factor which might have resulted in stuttering, but this other factor varied from case to case. This illustrates the difficulty which is encountered in attempts to study the effect

[1] Orton, *op cit*, p 195

[2] W Johnson and L Duke, 'Change of Handedness Associated with Onset or Disappearance of Stuttering: Sixteen Cases', *Journal of Experimental Education*, vol IV, No 2, 1935, pp 112-132

of changed handedness generally. It is unlikely that any two instances will be found where the only difference between them is that one is a case of changed handedness with stuttering, whereas the other is the same in all respects except that the preference for the left hand had remained undisturbed.

The investigators mentioned so far, if they have not considered change of handedness as the cause of stuttering, have all emphasised left-handedness, changed handedness or lack of preference as a factor of some importance in speech disorders, and in stuttering in particular. Other investigators have taken a different viewpoint, and have tended to belittle the importance of hand preference in the study of stuttering. Burt in *The Backward Child* made a study of the different percentages of stuttering found among left-handers, and claimed that the most significant fact about the figures is the wide divergence between different districts, indicating that it is not the mere fact of changing the handedness which affects speech, and saying that:

It is, therefore, difficult to withstand the inference that, in the main, it is the general severity of the school discipline—of which the insistence on right-handedness is but a sample—that is really responsible for an excess that appears equally evident in both the right-handed and the left-handed groups.[1]

He also cited the fact that in New Jersey schools where every child was required to use the right hand for writing, there was very little stuttering. The possibility is that inconsistency in the treatment of left-handers may be worse than almost any other treatment. This would explain the fact that stuttering is not increased where the policy for a certain district is consistent, that is, where the left-handed child knows and accepts that he must write with his right hand, as for example in New Jersey at the time referred to by Burt. If the policy of right-hand writing for all was not carried out by punishment of the left-handers but by a more rational approach no stuttering might result. The danger lies in the various interpretations put by different individuals on the suggestion that they 'encourage' right-handedness.

McAllister, though she did not ignore left-handedness or change of handedness in her patients, did not consider that it

[1] Burt, *op cit*, p 324

was a factor of major importance, and in support of her view cited the following figures: of 139 cases of stuttering, only 9 were left-handed, and only 2 of that number had been forced to become right-handed. Her discussion of one case in particular is of relevance to this problem:

> From the history of this case it appears that the cause of the stutter lay, not in the change from left- to right-handed movement, but in the severity of the treatment given to force the child to discard his left-handed habit. This severe treatment, meted out in the years of infancy on two separate occasions by two different people, seems to have roused, in a temperament by inheritance prone to excitability of the uncontrolled type, disturbing and upsetting emotion.[1]

The danger of over-emphasising the importance of change of handedness as a cause of stuttering is that it may lead to an apparent simplification of the problem, and may cause other factors of equal or greater importance to be ignored. The treatment and cure of stuttering is no easy task, and the danger of assuming that there is only one essential factor is that this narrows one's outlook and may cause vital factors to be overlooked in a particular individual. Thus, though changed handedness may be present in two cases of stuttering, its importance and significance in the two instances can be totally different, and the attitude of those in contact with the child and the emotional reactions of the child may be of considerably more importance than the actual fact of the change.

CONCLUSIONS

Certain limited conclusions can be drawn from the volume of research which has been carried out on handedness and its relationship to stuttering.

1 Changed handedness does not always result in stuttering. The fact that stuttering does not result in those who require to change from the preferred hand because of some accident is evidence that there is no absolute relationship between the two.

2 Stuttering may result from changed handedness, but whether it does or does not will depend to a great extent on the procedure adopted in effecting the change. The stuttering is not, however, a direct result of the change, in the sense that some upset of the neurological balance causes abnormal speech;

[1] McAllister, *op cit*, p 178

rather it is a possible manifestation of emotional disturbance resulting from the resistance by the child to the attempts to make him conform against his will to the wishes of the majority.

3 Certain periods appear to be critical with regard to speech development, and attempts to change handedness at these ages may have adverse effects on speech. It would seem to be desirable for the child to develop dominant handedness as early as possible, and any action which may delay that should be condemned, though, here again, the retarded speech and delay in acquiring dominant handedness may both result from some deeper neurological inadequacy.

4 All children have not the same tendency to develop a stutter even when the environmental circumstances are comparable; in children whose 'tolerance' is small, a change of handedness will accordingly have a considerable effect and may even act as the precipitating factor. There may be some weakness of the speech mechanisms in potential stutterers; this implies that while in such people stuttering is the reaction to extreme emotional circumstances, in others the reaction may be enuresis, or squinting—in each instance the weakest link.

It is clear that to gain a complete picture of stuttering attention must be paid, on the one hand, to the physiological aspects of the problem, in the form of a possible weakness or inadequacy of speech functioning, with a probable hereditary basis; and, on the other hand, to the psychological aspects, in the form of emotional stresses which precipitate the stuttering in a particular instance. Only among such stresses would changed handedness be included, and even then only as one possible precipitating factor. Undue emphasis of one aspect, such as changed handedness, is thus to be deplored.

CHAPTER VI

THE MEASUREMENT OF HANDEDNESS

NUMEROUS tests have been used in studies of handedness. Some investigators have attempted to find one reliable test and use that only, but the majority have employed a battery of tests, and have tried to build up a composite picture of handedness.

In many early investigations, where a comparison of handedness and some other factor was being made, e g, in many studies of the inheritance of handedness, the hand used for writing was often the only criterion. This invalidates the results, since pressure had frequently been applied, resulting in the use of the writing hand varying with the amount of compulsion imposed. A considerable number of left-handers may have been diverted to right-handedness at least in writing, the change-over being effected with some before school-age, when the writing habit was being established. Further, a correction for this under-estimation is made difficult because pressure towards right-handedness has varied from time to time, and from country to country.

The necessity to estimate the amount of 'covered' left-handedness is a problem which confronts any investigator of this trait, even when some criterion other than writing is adopted. Thus in many studies a battery of tests has been used in the hope that some of the tests at least would disclose the residue of left-handedness in those who had changed, or been changed to right-handedness, since there are some actions which even changed left-handers prefer to carry out, or perform better, with the left hand.

TYPES OF TESTS

I PREFERENCE

Preference may be measured in various ways. One or two important unimanual activities in which one hand can be used, or bimanual activities in which both are used but one hand plays the more important part, may be selected, and the subject's preferred hand for these determined. Two points arise in this connection: first, whether to select a small number of important activities or a large and varied number of tasks; second, whether these should be measured directly or indirectly, that is, whether the subject actually performs the selected activities or whether a questionnaire is used. These two considerations are bound up with each other, as the questionnaire enables a large number of subjects to be investigated on a variety of activities in a short time, whereas a great deal of time is required to apply tests directly. The importance of the selected activities in the total picture must be considered, as also must the reliability of the results.

An interesting analysis by Hull[1] of a questionnaire on handedness reveals how little reliance can be placed on the answers as indicative of the actual performance. She gave two questionnaires to students, each questionnaire having forty identical items, but arranged in a different order. The first was followed by a performance test which tested exactly what had been asked in the questionnaire, and in the same order. Four weeks later the second questionnaire was given and this was followed by a second performance test.

The following results were obtained:

1 Only fourteen of the forty items had a high reliability on the two questionnaires.

2 Only fourteen of the forty items were answered identically on the first questionnaire and the first performance test, in other words, were performed as the subject said he performed them.

3 On test and retest of performance and questionnaire, and comparison of written answer and performance, twelve items only were reliable.

These results show that little more reliable information is gained from a lengthy questionnaire than from a short test. The actual twelve items which gave a reliable figure in the questionnaire were those easily tested by performance, namely, hammering, cutting with scissors, card dealing, spinning a top,

[1] C J Hull, 'A Study of Laterality Test Items', *Journal of Experimental Education*, vol IV, 1936, pp 287-290

winding a watch, holding a toothbrush, sharpening a pencil, writing, cutting when eating, drawing, throwing, holding a tennis racquet.

With the exception of batting, the bimanual activities used by Hull, and often used by others, showed a low relationship between written answer and actual performance.

These results should make one wary of accepting statements on the subject of handedness, when these are given with no indication of the testing method employed. Many of the early statements were based on the results of such questionnaires circulated to thousands of subjects. Obviously such errors as these indicated will not be cancelled out by the use of large numbers of subjects. This may well be one explanation of the many contradictory statements on, and conflicting theories of, handedness.

A more satisfactory method of determining hand preference is to decide on a limited number of important activities, and devise suitable tests to measure preference in these, since it is impracticable to study handedness under everyday conditions. The tests should preferably be administered without the subject realising what is being tested, since otherwise the results may be distorted, especially with children who may choose one hand or other simply to please the investigator or to do what they think he expects.

Typical examples of important activities in which a choice of hand has to be made are writing, drawing, throwing, cutting, screwing and reaching. When dominance is determined by preference, it is important to take the precaution of seeing that neither hand is actually favoured by the arrangement of objects for the test. In addition it is advisable to give several trials, and to make a note of the preference at each attempt, as this will reveal the stability of the preference.

A common method of dealing with the results of such a battery of tests or the results of a questionnaire, is to apply such a formula as:

$$\frac{R + \dfrac{E \text{ or } B}{2}}{N}$$

where R is right preference,
E or B is either or both hands used,
and N is the number of items.

This is often referred to as the Dextrality Quotient, as a high score is indicative of extreme right-handedness, and a low score of left-handedness.[1]

II STRENGTH

The relative strength of the right and left hands is a doubtful measure of dominance as it is commonly understood. It is true that with the majority of people one hand has greater power than the other. Nevertheless there seems to be little connection between mere power and hand preference or ability in intricate movements or in an elaborate association of movements such as is necessary in the learning of handwriting. Many early studies used relative strength (as measured for example by a hand dynamometer) as an index of handedness, but the test is seldom used now, at least in isolation, though it is still included in some test batteries. Parson[2] in 1924 used it as his only test, while Woo and Pearson[3] in 1927 analysed Galton's material on handedness which was based on results of dynamometer testing. Roos[4] in 1935 used as a battery a tapping test, strength of grip and a number marking test. Burt mentions in *The Backward Child* that much of the evidence on primitive races was obtained on the basis of strength of grip. As he so rightly points out:

But the dynamometer is primarily a test of strength; whereas right- or left-handedness as I have defined it turns primarily on capacity for skill. I find that as many as forty-one per cent of those who habitually use the left hand for skilled actions nevertheless have a stronger grip with the right.[5]

The main criticisms of strength of grip as a measure of dominant handedness, especially with children are:

1 The dependence of the results on incentive gives such

[1] W Johnson and D Duke, 'The Dextrality Quotients of Fifty Six-year-olds with regard to Hand Usage', *Journal of Educational Psychology*, vol XXVII, 1936, pp 26-36; P A Witty and D Kopel, 'Sinistral and Mixed Manual-Ocular Behaviour in Reading Disability', *Journal of Educational Psychology*, vol XXVII, 1936, pp 119-134

[2] B S Parson, *Left-handedness—A New Interpretation*

[3] T L Woo and K Pearson, 'Dextrality and Sinistrality of Hand and Eye', *Biometrika*, vol XIX, 1927, pp 165-199

[4] M M Roos, 'Variations with Age in Frequency Distributions of Degrees of Handedness', *Child Development*, vol VI, No 4, 1935, pp 259-268

[5] Burt, *op cit*, footnote p 272

results as those of Binet and Vaschide (quoted in Whipple[1]), who found that the average grip was increased by about three kilograms, or by such an amount that the left hand surpassed the previous record of the right hand made without any incentive.

2 The actual differences between the scores with the left and right hands are relatively slight. Using Whipple's norms, the scores for an eight-year-old girl are: Right Hand 11·16 kg and Left Hand 10·48 kg, and for a six-year-old boy: Right Hand 9·21 kg and Left Hand 8·48 kg.

3 The tendency is for left-handed subjects to give stronger right-hand results. Whipple stated that some right-handed children may have a stronger grip with their left hand, and that according to Hrdlicka, nearly half the left-handed people make higher scores with the right hand. The left-handers with the stronger right-hand grip might be explained by the fact that changed left-handers have had practice in the use of the right hand, but the right-handers with the stronger left grip invalidate the dynamometer as a test of handedness.

Thus strength of one hand as compared with the other does not seem to be the basis on which hand preference rests.

III SPEED

Many tests of the relative motor abilities of the right and left hands have been used as a measure of dominance. The Tapping Test is one frequently employed, the usual method being to adapt a laboratory Tapping Test and allow the subject a certain period with each hand, taking the necessary precautions to eliminate practice effects. A calculation is then made of the relative number of taps performed by each hand, usually given as $\frac{L}{R}$ or $\frac{L}{R} \times 100$, which is an Index of Handedness; thus an index greater than unity or over one hundred indicates left-handedness.

The main criticism of such tests is that the effect of practice gained by one hand in writing (usually the right) will probably transfer considerably to tapping and such skills, and this transfer may cover any greater native ability in the other hand. However,

[1] G M Whipple, *Manual of Mental and Physical Tests* Part I, Baltimore: Warwick and York Inc, 1914, pp 100-109

if the relative grading of indices is considered, it is possible to distinguish the testees who are extremely right-handed from those whose left is almost as efficient as their right. This is of importance when considering whether a child should write with his left hand, or whether he may safely use his right. The Index of Handedness brings out the degree of handedness, but it does not show whether the subject is good with both hands or poor with both, which is after all an important consideration. To illustrate, a score of 60 with the left and 30 with the right gives an index of 2; but so also does a score of 20 and 10. Both indicate the same ratio of left-handedness, yet there is little similarity between the ability of the two subjects. The former, though he is left-handed, is better with his right hand, than the latter is with his left. If these were the scores of two children aged five, and the question was whether they could learn to write with the right hand, then obviously far more data than the actual index would be required. It is possible that the first child might be perfectly successful, while the second would present a different problem, and might suffer from poor motor co-ordination of both hands. In that case it might be as well to make the best of a bad job, and allow the second pupil to use his less bad hand, that is, his left. A more detailed discussion of this problem of changing handedness will be offered later. An Index of Handedness as calculated from a test of speed is evidently of practical value but it must be backed by details of the *actual* ability of each hand, and the results of other tests of handedness.

Roos[1] tested handedness at the kindergarten, high school and college levels. She claimed that the logarithmic handedness index (Log R/L) of a group of infants, as measured by the Tapping Test, is distributed normally, and does not form a bi-modal curve. She also stated that 75 per cent of those who have greater native ability with their left hand as indicated by a test such as the Tapping Test, develop preferential use of the right hand, probably because they live in a right-handed world, 81 per cent being found right-handed on the Tapping Test and 96 per cent on the Number Marking Test which involved writing. Since even a test of tapping will not reveal all cases of

[1] Roos, *op cit*, pp 259-268

native left-handedness, it seems safe to say, even as a conservative estimate, that there are more left-handed people using their right hand than their left, since even 19 per cent left-handed, as found on the Tapping Test, is more than twice the percentage writing with the left.

IV OTHER MOTOR TESTS

Other physical tests, less frequently used, which give a comparison of the relative motor performance with right and left hand, are the steadiness, aiming and tracing tests, detailed by Whipple.[1]

V SIMULTANEOUS BIMANUAL DRAWING

The early studies either omitted entirely subjects tested who were not revealed as definitely right- or left-handed or classified them by the hand most often preferred. Alternatively, some investigators arbitrarily determined intermediate classes, some making as many as seven, while others had three or four.[2] Obviously the numbers placed in the intermediate classes depend on the strictness of the criterion for right-handedness, the number of tests and of trials on each test. Without uniformity in these respects the results of one experimenter are not comparable with those of another, and the percentages of right-handed, left-handed and of ambidextrous individuals vary from experiment to experiment. Matters are made worse by the fact that in some of the reports the actual criteria are not stated.

The wide variations in percentages for right-handedness, left-handedness and ambidexterity given by different investigators do not necessarily imply, as some have supposed, that there is no such thing as a general trait of handedness, or that handedness is specific to the act performed. The masking may be the result rather of the right-handed influence of society, which makes it the socially acceptable procedure to use the right hand in preference to the left. Some actions are more affected by this social pressure than others, eg, writing and the

[1] Whipple, *op cit*, pp 147-160
[2] Witty and Kopel, *op cit*; R H Ojemann, 'Studies in Handedness: 1A-Technique for Testing Unimanual Handedness', *Journal of Educational Psychology*, vol XXI, 1930, pp 597-611; J M Rife, 'Types of Dextrality', *Psychological Review*, vol XXIX, 1922, pp 474-480; J E Downey, 'Laterality of Function', *Psychological Bulletin*, vol XXX, 1933, pp 109-142

handling of cutlery. Accordingly, if such actions are sampled by one's tests, the percentage of apparent left-handedness will fall, and that of right-handedness will rise correspondingly, or if ambidexterity is used as the classification for doubtful cases, then the number in this group will rise considerably.

In view of this confusion Van Riper[1] attempted to devise a new type of test, which he claimed would measure native handedness. He stated that an adequate test of laterality should fulfil these requirements:

1 It should show striking differences, and little overlapping.

2 It should have a high degree of reliability.

3 It should avoid as far as possible skills susceptible to previous environmental training.

4 It should show degrees of laterality, if these exist.

His original test involved drawing an asymmetrical pattern with both hands at the same time, on opposite sides of a vertical board. It was found that only one hand drew the diagram correctly, while the other made a mirror-image, that is, reversed the diagram. The hand which copied the diagram correctly was considered to be the dominant one, while that drawing a mirror-image was the non-dominant. This test was claimed by Van Riper to reveal instances of changed handedness, since it was possible for the hand used for writing to draw the diagram with clearer, bolder strokes, and yet actually do it in reverse, in which case it was shown to be in reality the non-dominant hand.

The Van Riper Laterality or Critical Angle Board was an elaboration of the vertical board idea in an attempt to measure degrees of laterality. The apparatus consists of a horizontal board with two vertical boards so placed on it that each can be rotated through 90 degrees. The testing is started with the vertical boards parallel to the chest, and paper so arranged on the vertical boards that the records for the right and left hands will be on opposite sides of the paper. The subject is seated with the apparatus at chest level, and is instructed to copy the diagram which is placed in front and at about 30 degrees above eye level, as shown in Figure 1 (facing p 60). The diagram has to be

[1] C Van Riper, 'A New Test of Laterality', *Journal of Experimental Psychology*, vol XVII, 1934, pp 305-313; 'The Quantitative Measurement of Laterality', vol XVIII, 1935, pp 372-382

copied with both hands at the same time and as quickly as possible, the eyes being kept fixed on the diagram all the time during the drawing. The vertical boards are rotated, the angle being increased thereby by 10 degrees at each trial, thus making the task more difficult each time, and the testing is repeated until a point is reached at which mirroring takes place with one hand. The experiment is then carried out with one further angle to check whether this is consistent. The first angle at which mirroring takes place is regarded as the critical angle, and if there is no mirroring with either hand when the boards are back to back the subject is classed as ambidextrous.

Van Riper used three types of pattern, Visual, Kinaesthetic and Script. With the Kinaesthetic Pattern, the subject learned the diagram first by tracing it with both hands by means of a stylus while blindfold. When the pattern had been learned in this manner, the subject was given two pencils, and made to repeat it on the apparatus, still with eyes closed. The Script Pattern was a word such as 'catch', which the subject had to write with both hands at the same time. Here again he was blindfold. These patterns were found to vary in difficulty, the Kinaesthetic Pattern giving the lowest Critical Angle, the Visual next, and the Script giving the highest.

The theoretic basis for this experiment, according to Van Riper, is the fact that the natural orientation of the two hands in simultaneous activity is in opposite directions, and the converging boards used in the experiment reveal this tendency. Increasing the angle increases distraction, and accordingly results in mirroring by the non-dominant hand.

To investigate the developmental trends through successive age groups Hildreth[1] made a study of the performance of young children in using both hands simultaneously for copying figures. She stated that the neuro-muscular apparatus favouring reversals is always potentially present, and that reversing the direction of the two hands in drawing the same figure simultaneously is a normal performance, which the higher intellectual processes can inhibit through learning or conscious attention. Hildreth found that with the five-year-old children there was little evi-

[1] G Hildreth, 'Bilateral Manual Performance, Eye Dominance and Reading Achievement', *Child Development*, vol XI, No 4, 1940, pp 311-317

FIGURE 1 The Van
Riper Critical Angle
Board

FIGURE 2 The Cone
Test of Eyedness
(Left-eyed Subject)

dence of conscious effort to make both hands move in the same direction, but that the tendency to mirror declined with age or, more accurately, with maturity. Thus the mirroring given by older children and adults on the Van Riper Test is probably to be explained as a result of the removal of the cues of vision and attention which normally inhibit such a performance.

Van Riper claimed that his test is the most reliable and best standardised test of handedness.[1] Evidence does not support such a sweeping contention, and in fact many criticisms can be passed on the test. Part of Van Riper's early investigation was carried out on two groups of subjects, one group being ambidextrous and the other a group of stutterers. He claimed that the stutterers gave results on his apparatus comparable to those of the ambidextrous subjects. The only real attempt by other investigators to evaluate the Critical Angle Board was that of Johnson and King,[2] who carried out an investigation on stutterers similar to that of Van Riper's. On the basis of their results they contested his claim for the apparatus. Adopting a procedure similar to that of Van Riper, they found:

1 that the correlation between the pattern scores and those obtained on a hand-usage questionnaire were low.

2 that using two groups, one of unselected stutterers, and one of unselected non-stutterers, the two groups were not definitely different in terms of their Critical Angle scores, or in terms of the hand with which the reversing was done.

From a comparison of their findings and those of Van Riper, they deduced that his highly right-handed and highly left-handed subjects were quite extreme groups, while his ambidextrous subjects were fairly representative of non-stutterers generally. They did point out, however, that from the Van Riper Test results a unimodal curve of handedness was obtained which tended to be strongly normal in form. There would only be a bimodal curve, such as is found on many tests of handedness, if there were two distinct types of handedness. They suggested the possibility that the more differentiating the measure, the more nearly will the scores obtained from a

[1] C Van Riper, 'The Quantitative Measurement of Laterality'; and *Speech Correction, Principles and Methods*

[2] W Johnson and A King, 'An Angle Board and Hand Usage Study of Stutterers and Non-Stutterers'

random population approximate to a normal distribution, and
that, if this is so, the theoretical significance of handedness as
traditionally considered would require to be re-examined.

Some of the defects of the Van Riper Test are inherent in the
nature of the test, while others arise from the testing technique
which could probably be overcome.[1]

In view of the unique nature of the Van Riper Test and the
fact that it is used in many clinics as a diagnostic instrument, it
is surprising that no systematic consideration has been given to
the contradictions indicated above nor any attempt made to
meet the more obvious objections. The apparatus has either
been accepted or condemned, the investigation by Johnson and
King being one of the few constructively critical studies. It
would nevertheless appear that some information which other
tests do not reveal can be obtained from a test such as that of
Van Riper. An example was the finding of Smith who made a
study of a group of retarded readers and a matched group of
successful readers. She found no significant difference between
the two groups on any one of an extensive battery of tests of
laterality including tests of handedness, eyedness and earedness.
She discovered, nevertheless, that:

> Retarded readers and reading achievers differ significantly in their
> performance on the Van Riper Test of 'Central' Dominance at the
> critical angle of 360 degrees. At this angle, the retarded readers reverse
> more often with the right hand; the reading achievers, with the left.[2]

It would consequently appear that the Van Riper Test should
not be summarily dismissed, since, as Van Riper himself admitted, it is at present crude, 'and any attempt to determine a
critical angle which would represent finally and forever the
exact state of a person's laterality would be foredoomed to
failure'.[3] Van Riper's Test, or one designed on similar principles, may still be of service in clinical diagnosis by revealing
whether confused laterality is a factor in cases of speech defects,
mirror-writing or backwardness in reading.

[1] *Infra*, Chapter XIV for more detailed study of the test
[2] L C Smith, 'A Study of Laterality Characteristics of Retarded Readers
and Reading Achievers', *Journal of Experimental Education*, vol XVIII, No
4, 1950, p 326
[3] C Van Riper, 'The Quantitative Measurement of Laterality'

CHAPTER VII

EYE DOMINANCE

DOMINANCE in eyedness is a conception quite different in character from dominance in handedness. Handedness difference is motor in nature, and unimanual activities are of far greater importance than bimanual. With eyedness on the contrary, binocular vision is obviously the commoner, and the more important, mode of vision.

Extreme views have been proposed on the importance of eye dominance. On the one hand, eye dominance has been claimed to be one aspect of sidedness, and actually the clearest manifestation of cerebral dominance. Gould stated that right-handedness follows generally on more perfect development of the right eye. 'Thus vision is the father of action, of right-handed action, and right-eyedness is bound up as a precedent, synchronous, and causal factor of right-handedness.'[1] Parson, though he modified Gould's view, also claimed that there was a close connection between eyedness and the preferred hand.[2] At the other extreme it has been maintained that there is no such thing as dominant eyedness and that it is a product or artefact of the tests, only arising under the artificial conditions of a laboratory experiment. It has been pointed out that our normal mode of vision is binocular, and that though we do on occasion have to sight with one eye, this is rather the exception. Warren and Clark, for example, have stated:

Eye dominance as a single unitary factor does not exist. Laterality of eye functioning is specifically determined by the situation in which the measurement is made. . . . Sensory neural organisation indicates that the problem of central functioning involves determining relationships of the two halves of the retina rather than the two eyes as a whole.[3]

[1] G M Gould, *Right-handedness and Left-handedness*, Philadelphia: J B Lippincott Co, 1908, p 103
[2] B S Parson, *Left-handedness—A New Interpretation*
[3] N Warren and B Clark, 'A Consideration of the Use of the Term Ocular Dominance', *Psychological Bulletin*, vol XXXV, 1938, p 302

More recently Walls[1] has made a similar statement, pointing out that though superficially each retina is a complete sense organ, neither eye moves alone except in a laboratory situation. These facts must be borne in mind when considering tests of eyedness especially those which purport to reveal, once and for all, the dominant sidedness, or cerebral dominance, of the subject.

Though many talk about the dominant eye, or the master eye, their meaning can vary considerably. Just as in handedness one can mean the better hand, or the preferred hand, so in eyedness, by the dominant eye can be meant either the eye with better visual acuity, that is, which can actually see better, or the preferred eye. Further, dominance can arise in binocular vision when one eye is being used by itself, or when one eye takes the leading role in fixating or sighting.

TYPES OF TESTS FOR EYE DOMINANCE

I SIGHTING PREFERENCE IN MONOCULAR VISION

In spite of the fact that binocular vision is the normal type, some investigators, to determine the preferred eye for sighting, have used tests where a deliberate choice of one eye has to be made. Examples of such tests are: sighting through a tube, looking through a small hole, sighting along a toy gun.[2] The type of situation in everyday life where such a choice has to be made is in shooting with a rifle, or in using a microscope. Care must be taken in tests of eyedness to eliminate as far as possible the effects of the dominant hand; thus the subject should not hold the apparatus, or if he does, it must be held with both hands. When such precautions are observed, the correlation between handedness and eyedness is low.

II VISUAL ACUITY

In some early studies of eyedness, visual acuity was the only measure of dominance used. Woo and Pearson,[3] in reporting

---

[1] G L Walls, 'A Theory of Ocular Dominance', *AMA Archives of Ophthalmology*, vol XLV, No 4, 1951, pp 387-412
[2] B Crider, 'Unilateral Sighting Preference', *Child Development*, vol VI, No 2, 1935, pp 163-164
[3] T L Woo and K Pearson, 'Dextrality and Sinistrality of Hand and Eye'

on Galton's material, stated that the measure used was the superiority of the right over the left eye, measured by the distance in inches at which type could be read with each eye separately. It has since been pointed out by Downey[1] and others that comparative visual acuity should not be confused with eye dominance. Further, the results of Gahagan[2] have shown that in only 55 per cent of his cases where there was a difference of acuity, was the eye with the better acuity the preferred one, and he therefore concluded that dominance and acuity were independent visual phenomena. It may be that in the majority of people the difference in visual acuity is actually of too slight a degree to be of importance. Gahagan found that 40 per cent of his subjects had visual acuity equal or almost equal for the two eyes. However, when the dominant eye has less than normal acuity and the non-dominant eye is better than normal, as Gahagan found in a number of cases, the individuals concerned have a pronounced lack of visual efficiency. Recently studies have been made by Spache,[3] Robinson[4] and Smith[5] on the connection of visual acuity and dominance with reading difficulties. Obviously reading efficiency may be lowered if the dominant eye is of under-average efficiency. It does not seem possible, however, to train the non-dominant eye to become dominant. So far as the connection between visual acuity and dominance is concerned, it is at least clear that though the better eye may be the preferred one, visual acuity is not the basis of eye preference.

III SIGHTING PREFERENCE IN BINOCULAR VISION

Under normal conditions when both eyes are apparently functioning it is not evident that one eye is dominant. Some of the tests of eye dominance require the subject to have both eyes

[1] J E Downey, 'Laterality of Function'

[2] L Gahagan, 'Visual Dominance-Acuity Relationships', *Journal of General Psychology*, vol IX, 1933, pp 455-459

[3] G Spache, 'A Binocular Reading Test', *Journal of Applied Psychology*, vol XXVII, 1943, pp 109-113

[4] *Clinical Studies in Reading I*; Supplementary Educational Monographs, Chicago: University of Chicago Press, 1949, Chapter V

[5] L C Smith, 'A Study of Laterality Characteristics of Retarded Readers and Reading Achievers'

open; he is then under the impression that he is using both but the situation necessitates the use of only one.

One of the simplest tests of dominance when both eyes are apparently in operation, is a sighting test, either through a cone or through a small hole in a piece of paper. The subject is instructed to take the cone in both hands and hold it up to his eyes. He is then directed to look through it directly at the experimenter, keeping both eyes open. Such is the situation that only one eye is actually sighting, and that eye is seen by the experimenter through the end of the cone, as illustrated in Figure 2 (facing p 60). A similar technique is employed when using a card with a small hole in the centre. The card is held in both hands, at arms' length, while the subject, with both eyes open, fixates an object held by the experimenter. Here again, the eye seen through the hole is the dominant one. If the subject were asked to close the dominant eye, without moving the paper or the cone, he would see nothing, whereas closing the non-dominant has no effect. This is the basis of various other tests where the subject looks at an object along his finger, or through a ring with both eyes open; he closes one eye, then the other. When the dominant eye is closed, the object appears to move, while closing the non-dominant has no effect. This is explained by the fact that he is actually, and can only be, fixating with one eye, since there is only one sight-line that joins the point, from one eye to the point of the pencil or finger, and then to the object. The advantage of using some test such as the 'cone' or 'hole in card' is that the investigator sees for himself which is the dominant eye, and does not have to rely on the subject's report; this is obviously advantageous, especially in testing children. It also makes it possible to test children for eye dominance at a very early age. More elaborate apparatus on similar principles has been devised by Parson,[1] Cuff,[2] Lund[3] and others. Parson used a small darkened box which he called a 'Manuscope', which had movable shutters to permit blocking of either eye. Cuff measured the amount of dominance by an elaboration of

[1] Parson, op cit
[2] N B Cuff, 'A Study of Eyedness and Handedness', *Journal of Experimental Psychology*, vol XIV, 1931, pp 164-175
[3] F H Lund, 'The Monoptometer: A New Device for Measuring Eye-Dominance', *American Journal of Psychology*, vol XLIV, 1932, pp 181-183

the manuscope. Using his 'Manoptometer', and an easel arrangement whereby the subject, as with Parson's Manuscope, fixated a picture, Cuff brought from the side into the field of vision a second picture, and asked the subject to say when he could see it. He repeated this, bringing the picture in from the other side. The back of the easel was marked off in centimeters, which, according to Cuff, made it possible to secure quantitative results. Miles[1] used a much simpler measure of dominance which he termed a V-Scope, which was similar to the cone described earlier, and claimed that with this simple test the reliability was high.

A warning was given by Crider[2] about placing too great reliance on the findings of so-called tests of dominance. He sought to account for the wide variation in the results of different studies of eyedness by pointing out that in over a hundred studies of ocular dominance which had appeared, right-eyedness varied from 55 to 90 per cent, left-eyedness from 6 to 33 per cent, and impartial eyedness from zero to 26 per cent. This he claimed was the result of the different criteria adopted by investigators. Using a variety of common unilateral sighting tests Crider gave his subjects forty-five opportunities of sighting, and designated them as right-eyed if they were right on all the tests, left-eyed only if left at all trials, while any variation he listed as impartial-eyed. If one sighting opportunity is given, obviously subjects are designated right or left only, therefore leaving no impartial-eyed, but Crider found that as the number of sighting opportunities increased, so did the impartial-eyed, being 13 per cent with six trials, and 50 per cent with forty-five trials. From this he concluded that by increasing the opportunities indefinitely, a point will eventually be reached where, theoretically, all subjects will be impartial-eyed. That assumes that the limit had not been reached with the testing he did. It is possible that dominance in the remaining 50 per cent was stable and would not vary, no matter what test was used nor how many opportunities were given. In view of Crider's findings it is nevertheless worth remembering his statement that:

---

[1] W R Miles, 'Ocular Dominance, Demonstrated by Unconscious Sighting', *Journal of Experimental Psychology*, vol XII, 1929, pp 113-126
[2] Crider, *op cit*, pp 163-164

In brief any investigator can take any set of data and by varying the criterion of consistency can vary the percentage of eye preference. Consequently the data of no two investigators are comparable unless the number of sighting opportunities and the criterion are stated, and are in accord.[1]

Crider's findings are supported by those of Buxton and Crosland, who gave four tests of eyedness to their subjects, and worked out the correlation between the tests. The tests used were the Manuscope, Hole in card, Sighting and Aiming, these being regarded as representative of the various eyedness tests utilised by experimenters. From their results they concluded that:

1 typical simple tests of eye-preference, when repeated in slightly varying ways a relatively large number of times, prove to be statistically reliable; and

2 the existence of a 'unitary' trait of eye-preference as such is not indicated. The latter finding may be interpreted to mean that a whole battery, not a single example of eye-preference tests, is necessary to determine which is the eye most likely to be preferred. As previously mentioned, clinicians and experimentalists who have determined eye-preference by a single test or very few tests should take into account the fact that no one test is sufficient to show various degrees of preference. It may be that eye-preference, as hand-preference, is better defined in terms of the number of activities for which the eye is preferred.[2]

Crider[3] planned an investigation to decide whether unilateral sighting-preferences were related to characteristic differences in the ocular muscle balance of the two associated eyes. He studied the speed, direction, and extent of movement in one eye with respect to similar movements in the opposing eye, and found that the eye with muscle insufficiency, as he defined it, was seldom the sighting or dominant eye.

IV THE PHI TEST OF EYE DOMINANCE

The Phi Test[4] of Jasper and Raney was claimed by them to

[1] Crider, *op cit*, p 164

[2] C E Buxton and H. R Crosland, 'The Concept of Eye-Preference', *American Journal of Psychology*, vol XLIX, 1937, p 461

[3] B Crider, 'The Relationship of Eye Muscle Balance to the Sighting Eye', *Journal of Experimental Psychology*, vol XVIII, 1935, pp 152-154

[4] Phi-phenomenon—the appearance of motion from stationary stimuli when they are presented successively in two neighbouring positions. H C Warren, *Dictionary of Psychology*.

determine 'unilateral dominance as opposed to the peripheral ocular aspects of the visual-perceptive system.'[1] Two lights were used in the experiment, and were so arranged that conditions for the perception of the Phi-movement were simultaneously presented to both eyes. When the subject was instructed to fixate the near light, a double image was seen instead of the far light; similarly when the far light was fixated, the near light appeared as a double image on either side of the fixated light. While the subject watched the near light, the far one was switched off, and when it was again switched on, the fixated light appeared to move. Since stimulation was equal for perception of movement both to the right and to the left simultaneously, movement seen only in one direction would, according to Jasper and Raney, indicate a lateral dominance in some part of the visual mechanism. They further claimed that from the direction of movement could be deduced not only the side of dominance, but also whether it was ocular or central dominance.

The Phi Test of dominance is very elaborate and takes a considerable time to administer, some subjects not seeing the movement for fifteen to twenty-five minutes. In addition, the correlation of this test with tests of monocular sighting is very low. For these reasons it would be well to avoid the use of such a test, except for experimental purposes, since the type of eye dominance revealed by it has not been shown to be any more fundamental than the more readily observed types.

V RETINAL-RIVALRY TESTS

In retinal-rivalry tests the eye whose image is in consciousness for the longer time in a retinal-rivalry situation is regarded as dominant. This can be measured by means of a stereoscope where a different view is presented to each eye, and the subject sees each alternately. Washburn, Faison and Scott made a comparison of the results of this type of test and a Cone test, and found that in only 33·3 per cent of the subjects was there consistency between the results of the two tests. They claimed for the rivalry test that it 'is quite possibly freer from the

[1] H H Jasper and E T Raney, 'The Phi Test of Lateral Dominance', *American Journal of Psychology*, vol XLIX, 1937, pp 450-457

handedness factor and certainly gives a finer scale of measurement, since the results can be expressed in the difference between percentages of time during which each of the fields is dominant'.[1]

Walls pointed out in connection with the Phi Test and tests of Retinal-Rivalry, that they are 'asymmetries without the least possibility of an oculomotor element',[2] and could not agree with dominance of one hemisphere of the brain except by chance, but that at least the phi and rivalry phenomena show that there is at least one kind of 'ocular dominance' that is not connected with dominance of the hemispheres of the brain and is in no way related to the asymmetry underlying sighting dominance. A new explanation of eye dominance called 'Directional Dominance' has been offered by Walls. He maintained that the binocular percepts of visual direction are formed from the innervations to the muscles of one eye only; further, that the directions followed in localising a visual point are governed by this one eye, whether the eye sees the given point or not, and that the motor activities of the other eye are not made use of in space perception. He illustrated this theory by diagrams claiming that it explains all the properties of the dominant eye in binocular vision and of the dominance of one when one alone is used.

Many people do not know their dominant eye, and while learning to use a microscope, for instance, have a period of experimenting with alternate eyes and finally settle down to the use of one. In using a microscope, there is the possibility that it is not so much the dominance of the one eye as the suppression of the other which is of importance. Nevertheless, the eye selected is the dominant eye, not by virtue of the fact that it has received practice, for the practice has merely revealed the dominance. It is interesting to note in this connection a fact pointed out by Walls, that after practice, the microscopist becomes able to keep both eyes open, without thereby distracting his attention from the slide. If, when using the microscope, he should attempt to use the other eye, the contents of the field of

[1] M F Washburn, C Faison and R Scott, 'A Comparison between the Miles A-B-C Method and Retinal Rivalry as Tests of Ocular Dominance', *American Journal of Psychology*, vol XLVI, 1934, p 636
[2] Walls, *op cit*, pp 387-412

view of the dominant eye seem to interfere with good observation of the slide. Miles pointed out this phenomenon earlier,
when he suggested that ocular dominance clears the field by
'giving the right of way to the image that belongs to the dominant eye, making it appear more substantial than the other
which then tends to be more or less suppressed'.[1]

This survey of the commonest tests of eyedness reveals the
range of factors considered important by various investigators,
and indicates also the importance of caution in the acceptance
of the findings from such tests. In spite of this it must be
inferred that eye dominance is a reality, though some of the
statements on the subject have been rash and many of the
findings of dubious validity.

[1] Miles, op cit, p 113

CHAPTER VIII

CROSSED LATERALITY

CROSSED LATERALITY OF HAND AND EYE

WHEN the dominant hand and eye are not in accord, the condition is termed crossed laterality. Many have suggested that the ideal arrangement is for the favoured hand and the dominant eye to be on the same side, as this would facilitate co-ordination of movements. Since eye dominance, unlike dominant handedness, is not evident to the casual observer, and accordingly not subjected to social pressure, it is regarded by some as the better indication of true laterality, and crossed laterals (at least of the right-handed and left-eyed type) are thought to be native left-handers. From the view that like-dominance is the natural arrangement and also the ideal has arisen the belief that crossed laterality is an educational handicap, and that it may even be the cause of backwardness in reading and of various behaviour disorders. A critical assessment of such statements is not possible without some knowledge of the actual findings on the correlation between handedness and eyedness in the normal population, and for that reason, several of the more important studies will be mentioned.

In 1908 Gould[1] gave expression to the most extreme view of the relationship between handedness and eyedness claiming that for speed, accuracy and co-ordination the centres for right-eyedness, right-handedness, speech and writing must be in the left cerebral hemisphere. No evidence has yet been adduced in support of the view that eye-dominance is in any way connected with one side of the brain, let alone connected with the same side as handedness. Parson somewhat modified Gould's view stating:

Man has also developed certain dominant *single* faculties such as

---

[1] G M Gould, *Right-handedness and Left-handedness*

speech and memory which cannot be classed as belonging to either side of the body exclusively, but rather to the organism as a whole. In a general way it can be stated that we find the neural areas which innervate these highly complex single faculties *grouped in the same hemisphere* that contains *the centre controlling handedness and eyedness.* This affords the most direct and speedy co-ordination of sight impressions with intellect, will and action.[1]

Parson then attempted to test, or rather to justify, his hypothesis by examining the handedness and eyedness of his subjects, using strength of grip as a measure of handedness, and testing eyedness by means of his Manuscope. He did not find, as he expected, a perfect correlation, but on analysing the cases of disagreement he claimed to have substantiated his hypothesis. Where crossed laterality was of the nature of right-hand, left-eye, he found that the subject had originally shown left-handed tendencies, whereas in those who were left-handed and right-eyed, he found some ocular defect in the left eye to explain this unexpected preference. He made no analysis, however, of the cases of agreement, where he might have found just as many changed left-handers. Parson's findings have not been confirmed by any subsequent investigator, and Cuff[2] actually repeated the experiment with Parson's instrument, and found that the exceptions to Parson's theory of handedness as a result of eyedness amounted to approximately 20 per cent of the number tested. In other words, crossed dominance is common.

Woo and Pearson[3] investigated this problem more scientifically to learn if the amount of frequency of ocular dextrality bears any relation to the amount of frequency of manual dexterity. Their data were wholly opposed to the view of a master eye. On the tests they used, relative strength of grip and relative visual acuity, they did not even find any evidence of a correlation between the two. In such studies the tests used must be considered, as they frequently give a clue to differences in the findings.

The studies mentioned were all made on adults, but more recently tests have been applied to school children, and even to

---

[1] B S Parson, *Left-handedness—A New Interpretation*, p 22
[2] N B Cuff, 'The Interpretation of Handedness', *Journal of Experimental Psychology*, vol XI, 1928, pp 27-39
[3] T L Woo and K Pearson, 'Dextrality and Sinistrality of Hand and Eye'

pre-school children. Cuff[1] studied 237 children and 109 college students, and found that all the left-handed children were left-eyed with one exception, who was equal-eyed. One cannot, however, infer from this that all the left-eyed were left-handed; in fact Cuff also stated that the correlation between eyedness and handedness is apparently low.

A recent study of pre-school children which enables one to note the correspondence of handedness and eyedness before the writing situation has affected hand preference is that of Updegraff,[2] who made a study of seventy-four children aged from two to six years old, using an adaptation of the Miles Cone and a handedness test of her own. Her findings were as follows:

Right-handed children who are Right-eyed—72 per cent.
Left-handed children who are Left-eyed—66 per cent.
Right-eyed children who are Right-handed—95 per cent.
Left-eyed children who are Left-handed—21 per cent.

She pointed out that a right-eyed child is evidently more likely to be right-handed than a left-eyed child to be left-handed. Her figures accord fairly closely with those found by other investigators working on older subjects. In summing up her findings she also stated:

There is the possibility that even at these early ages 'native handedness', if it exists, has been changed through training in some cases. . . . Possibly the concept of unilaterality as varying in degree and of that degree expressed in terms of different manifestations of dominance, of which handedness and eyedness are only two, is the most plausible hypothesis at present.[3]

It is clear from the various studies of dominance in normal subjects that crossed laterality with regard to hand and eye is much commoner than is often realised, the figures being about 70 per cent uncrossed and 30 per cent crossed, with the majority of the latter right-handed and left-eyed. While it is possible that there exists in this latter group a number of changed left-handers, this cannot account for the whole group. Further, one cannot assume that all changed left-handers are left-eyed—

---

[1] N B Cuff, 'A Study of Eyedness and Handedness'
[2] R Updegraff, 'The Correspondence between Handedness and Eyedness in Young Children', *Pedagogical Seminary*, vol XLII, 1933, pp 490-492
[3] *Ibid*, p 492

some may be right-eyed; it is quite legitimate to suggest that they might owe their success in effecting the necessary shift to the fact that they were already right-dominant with regard to one aspect, eyedness.

Although it is established that crossed laterality is common, this does not exclude the view that unilateral dominance is the ideal. It has frequently been asserted that it is an advantage to have the preferred hand and eye on the same side, as was assumed in the theories of Gould and Parson. If this were so, it would be of importance, particularly in education, since it has a bearing on the problem of whether a left-handed child who has been changed to right-handedness should be encouraged to change back or not. If the child were right-eyed then it might be advisable to allow him to continue using his right hand; whereas if he were left-eyed, and of changed handedness, this would result in his labouring under the double disadvantage of using the non-preferred hand, and also the hand on the side opposite to the preferred eye. At present no decision can be given on this issue since it is not known in what activities crossed laterality may be a disadvantage. Its effect may be limited to certain situations, for example, monocular sighting in such activities as rifle shooting. Whether it is important in binocular situations is not established. The educational aspects of this problem will be dealt with later, but mention may be made here of a study by Lund,[1] on the connection between eye dominance and eye-hand co-ordination. He used a test in which eye-hand co-ordination was obviously important for skilled performance, an accuracy test similar to that in Whipple's *Manual of Mental and Physical Tests*.[2] The subject attempted to strike accurately crosses marked on a target placed at such a distance that his pencil would touch it when his arm was outstretched. Lund compared the results when both eyes were open, when only the dominant was open and when only the non-dominant was open. He found that the best scores were gained with both eyes open, and the poorest with only the non-dominant open. However, it is interesting to note:

[1] F H Lund, 'The Dependence of Eye-Hand Co-ordination upon Eye-Dominance', *American Journal of Psychology*, vol XLIV, 1932, pp 756-762
[2] Pp 147-151

In the case of the left-eyed dextrals the non-dominant eye yielded the better score in almost as many cases as the dominant eye. This would seem to indicate that the right eye, though not the dominant eye in the case of these subjects, has nevertheless been brought more into use than might otherwise have been the case, since it is the nearer eye so far as the functionally dominant hand is concerned. The data in this case point definitely to the advantage of consistent lateralism.[1]

Thus we may say that crossed laterality appears in the normal population in the ratio of approximately 3:7, and that certain actions may be facilitated by having consistent laterality, though we have no proof that it is of sufficient importance to warrant attempting to change dominance in order that there may be accord. The suggestion that the left-eyed dextrals may have been native sinistrals who were changed to right-handedness appears to be an unlikely explanation of the whole group, though it may explain certain cases, and these may in fact be the ones where crossed laterality is a handicap. Not only are they using the non-preferred hand, but that on the opposite side from the dominant eye. Confusion is possible in these cases. Finally, a tentative suggestion is the possibility that pure sinistrals (LH-LE) and pure dextrals (RH-RE), may be extremes and that crossed laterals (LH-RE and RH-LE) may be intermediates even with regard to handedness, and perhaps a change is also easier with them for that reason. This possibility has been mentioned recently by Humphrey, who made a study of the variability of hand preference for different activities. From the results which he obtained on the basis of a questionnaire given to male students, he graded the subjects for handedness, giving them an index to represent the degree of left-handedness. When he studied the eye preferences of his left-handed subjects, he found that:

Total unilaterality is relatively more frequent in the control group than in the left-handed subjects. Of the latter, the more strongly left-handed show an appreciably higher incidence of left-eyedness (27 out of 38, ie 71 per cent) than the less strongly so (14 out of 32, ie 44 per cent). Ambilaterals and others whose laterality index is less that ·75 show an almost equal division between left-eyedness and right-eyedness.[2]

---

[1] Lund, *op cit*, p 762
[2] M E Humphrey, 'Consistency of Hand Usage', *British Journal of Educational Psychology*, vol XXI, 1951, pp 220-221

Some caution must be shown in accepting these results as final, as no actual test of eyedness was given to the subjects, the results being based on a statement in the questionnaire. Further, the two groups of left-handers were constituted on the basis of writing with the left hand, the extreme group writing with the left hand, while the other group comprised those who were left-handed in other important activities but not in writing. Since many of these students started school at a time when left-hand writing was frowned upon even more than it is to-day, one cannot be certain that Humphrey's group of less extreme left-handers were natively less extreme; many in that group may have been forced to write with the right hand.

Many of the findings on crossed laterality admit of numerous interpretations, and other interpretations than those put forward by the investigators into handedness, eyedness, and the connection between the two, for many of them have set out with a hypothesis which they wished to substantiate, and in their desire or anxiety to do so, have seized upon all confirming evidence and ignored or overlooked the negative results, or dismissed them as caused by defects in sampling.

OTHER ASPECTS OF CROSSED LATERALITY

When reference is made to crossed laterality, hand and eye dominance is usually implied, although two equally valid aspects are hand and foot preferences, or indeed any other pair of structures in which asymmetrical functioning may be displayed. Attention has more frequently been directed to crossed laterality of hand and eye because of its potentialities for educational disability. Studies have nevertheless been carried out by Cuff,[1] Eyre and Schmeckle[2] and Dart,[3] to mention only a few, on the relationship between hand and foot preferences, and with fewer contradictory results than were evident in those on hand and eye. Investigators, though finding a low correlation between hand and eye preference, have usually found a high

[1] N B Cuff, 'A Study of Eyedness and Handedness'
[2] M B Eyre and M M Schmeckle, 'A Study of Handedness, Eyedness and Footedness', *Child Development*, vol IV, 1933, pp 73-78
[3] C Dart, 'The Hand, Eye and Foot Preference of Two Hundred Mentally Subnormal Subjects and Two Hundred Subjects of Normal or Superior Intelligence', *Psychological Bulletin*, vol XXXI, 1934, p 593

correlation between hand and foot. The findings in this connection will not be discussed in detail as crossed laterality of these is comparatively rare, and in some cases exemplified by right hand and left foot preference resulting from change of handedness. Left-footers have their obvious sphere of usefulness, but possibly ability to use either foot is of more value in sport. The aspects of footedness most commonly tested are kicking, stepping and hopping, which do not require for their performance such a high degree of skill and precision as manual activities, and for that reason foot preference is not so consistent as is hand preference. 'Kicking' is the most consistently performed foot activity, and, as might be expected, the one which correlates most highly with handedness.

CHAPTER IX

LEFT-HANDEDNESS AND WRITING PROBLEMS

GENERAL DISCUSSION

UNTIL very recently only a small minority of those with left-hand preference were actually using the left hand for writing, though many of them were using it for almost every other skilled action. Some adults, even though forbidden to use the left hand for writing at school, have after leaving school changed over to writing with the left hand of their own accord and rapidly acquired great facility. Others in spite of years of training are so poor or ill-at-ease with the right hand that, within a few months of changing, their left hand surpasses the right in skill. From this it can be inferred that many strongly left-handed children are not writing with the left hand. Thus the group of left-hand writers is peculiarly constituted, a fact which should be borne in mind when any comparison is being attempted between left-hand writers and right-hand writers, since the latter group contains many extremely left-handed people. The efforts to change left-handed children to the use of their right hand have varied in strength from year to year, district to district, school to school, and even from one family to another. One of the most unfortunate aspects of the treatment meted out to left-handers has been its inconsistency, not only from one child to another, but also with an individual child. What happens frequently is that in the infant classes no objection is raised to the child using his left hand; but for nearly every pupil there comes a stage in his school career—often about the age of eight at the time he should be acquiring some speed in his writing—when a teacher suggests to the child, or insists, that he try the other hand. Sometimes he is made to feel so awkward and different that he changes over of his own accord; this is more frequent with girls. As

G   79

a result of such a transfer one of three things may happen:

1 If the child is fairly skilful with both hands, he may find that he manages to acquire right-hand writing of a standard which is not far short of that of his right-handed companions. If this occurs the transfer has been successful; since its ill-effects on the child are probably negligible, and it makes the teacher's task easier. To this category belong many who are commonly termed ambidextrous. They are not necessarily of equal skill with both hands, but are of above-average skill with the right hand and can therefore hold their own with their right-handed fellows. In addition they are extremely 'dextrous' with the left hand, and remain so in spite of the fact that it receives less training. Many investigators have maintained that there is no true ambidexterity, and that those to whom the name 'ambi-dextrous' is given are, in reality, changed left-handers. Some people, in spite of a left preference, change over to the right hand before or when they start to write, but those who appear ambidextrous even in writing frequently started writing with the left hand, and were later successfully changed to the right. Mention might be made in passing of a cult at the beginning of this century initiated by Jackson who founded the 'Ambi-dextral Cultural Society' for the promotion of educational reform and two-handed training. Jackson even advocated that children should be trained to use both hands simultaneously in writing, and, as a final step, taught to write different things with both hands at the same time. His book *Ambidexterity* is a rather extravagant but entertaining advocacy of the benefits to be derived from becoming equally skilled with both hands.[1] As a result of Jackson's work many infant schools introduced two-handed training and copy books were even prepared for this, but the craze did not survive long. Its main interest now is that it accounts for the view held so often by people of a certain age-group that ambidexterity is the ideal.

2 The second group with a left preference are in quite a different position. Many children, having once changed to the right hand, either because of excessive pressure or a desire to conform to custom, do not attempt to use the left again for writing, though they may be very much poorer with the right

[1] J Jackson, *Ambidexterity*, London: Kegan Paul and Co Ltd, 1905, p 244

than the majority of right-handers, and also poorer than they are with their left. Many of these are found in the category of bad writers. This cannot be advanced as the sole, or even a principal, cause of bad writing in general, but it is safe to say that it is the explanation in a number of cases of illegible or slow writing. These people might have been good writers had they been permitted to use the left hand, as also might many left-handers if they had not been forced to use the right hand from infancy. Orton, when discussing cases of special writing disability, stated in this connection:

The second type of this disability is that in which the quality of the writing suffers. In speed, these latter children are variable; some of them are slow, as well as poor writers, while others achieve a good speed but the quality of their product is far from acceptable and often quite illegible.

In many cases of this difficulty there is a history of a shift from the left to the right hand in early infancy, or an enforced training of the right hand for writing in spite of a strong preference for the left as exhibited in all spontaneously acquired skills. These shifted sinistrals seem a little more apt to fall into the group of slow writers rather than poor writers, although there is no consistency in this.[1]

3 We must also consider those who write with the left hand, but who for a period of weeks or months, probably about the age of eight, and at the instigation of a teacher, attempted to write with the right hand. At some time or other most left-hand writers are compelled by someone to use the other hand. For many it is only after a period of such experimenting, which causes not only a delay in acquiring speed with the left hand but also a sense of failure and frustration that they are allowed to revert to their preferred hand. Thus, many left-hand writers write with the left hand only on sufferance. Several such pupils when asked why they changed back to the left, have replied 'When the teacher saw I was worse with my right hand, I was allowed to change back to the left'. The danger is that these children are retarded in school as a result of struggling to write with the poorer hand for a period, and what is worse, they have a sense of failure if they do not succeed in learning to write with the right hand. It is no triumph for them to be permitted to revert to their preferred hand; on the contrary, the preferred

[1] *Op cit*, p 101

hand is only tolerated because they failed to adapt to the other.

When estimating the truth of statements on left-handedness and its connection with writing the following points should be borne in mind:

1 Not all those with an innate preference for the left hand write with that hand. Many who are proficient with the left are yet sufficiently proficient with the right to have adapted to right-hand writing.

2 Most left-handers, even those writing with the left hand, have been subjected at some time to a period of enforced use of the right hand.

3 The inconsistency in the treatment of left-handedness means that the background of *each* individual must be studied, since some have a struggle before they are permitted to use the left hand while others are automatically permitted to use it provided they show a strong preference for it. Thus, comparisons between groups of left-handers should be regarded with caution, while comparisons between right- and left-handed groups as far as writing is concerned are actually dangerous.

It must be admitted that there is some truth in the suggestion that left-handers are bad writers. It is, however, a generalisation with only a certain amount of truth in it, and for that reason all the more dangerous, since frequently wrong conclusions are drawn from it. By no means *all* left-hand writers are bad writers, on the contrary, some are as legible and as speedy as the better right-hand writers, though their style may be different. The majority of those writing with the left hand produce writing which is either neat or speedy, but seldom both; this is admittedly a failing not entirely confined to them. They do, however, suffer more from fatigue when subjected to prolonged periods of writing than those using the right hand.

COMMON CHARACTERISTICS OF WRITING WITH THE LEFT HAND

I THE ACTUAL WRITING

Most left-handers, given time, can write neatly; their most common failing is their inability to acquire the necessary speed to meet everyday requirements. This is not, however, a necessary characteristic of writing with the left hand, but only a failing commonly found as a result of lack of proper guidance. The slope of their writing is seldom naturally the orthodox forward slant, and where this has been insisted upon by the school, the slant frequently varies from letter to letter, and from page to page. No definite style is acquired, it is as if a left-hand writer were still seeking some new adjustment or more comfortable technique, even at the adult stage. The writing of left-handed children is often messy and when written in ink is frequently smudged. This is not so true of the adult left-hander who usually develops some technique whereby this is avoided, but often success is attained only at the cost of considerable strain.

II POSITION WHEN WRITING

When writing is done with the left hand, an awkward position is frequently adopted. A cramped position of the arm and twisted position of the whole body is very common, as also is an awkward tense grip of the pen or pencil. Left-handers seem to remain conscious of the writing movement for a long time; they have accordingly jerky, effortful movements when writing. They use many odd methods of writing. A warning is nevertheless necessary in this connection, since *those who write in an odd manner are those who are noticed*, while other left-handers writing in a normal easy way are seldom apparent to the casual observer. Thus people are inclined to generalise from the few awkward left-handers they have noticed, and to assume that awkwardness is a characteristic of left-handedness. A considerable number of left-handers do, however, have some peculiar method of writing. This is true not only of adults who grew up at a time when left-handedness was even less tolerated than it is now, but is also true of young children in schools today. There are various types of peculiarity in the way the pen is held, the commonest being 'the hook', where the hand is actually above the line of writing, as shown in Figure 3 (a). In fact this position is so common that it is even regarded by many teachers as the normal method of writing with the left hand. There is nothing normal about this position, and some consideration of the differences between writing with the right and with the left hand readily explains how it develops. When one writes with the right hand, the hand is ahead of the writing; while to achieve this when writing with the left hand, the writing would require to be done from right to left. Thus a left-handed child finds when he starts writing that the grip which the teacher demonstrates and which his right-handed neighbour takes of the pencil is not suitable, and since he is shown no alternative, he adopts a grip of his own. He must so grip the pencil that he can see what he is writing; and he therefore grips it at the same distance from the point as does the right-hander, but curves his hand slightly to enable him to see under it. This device is fairly satisfactory with pencil writing, but when he begins to write with ink he finds it is no longer satisfactory for two reasons: first, the point of the pen pokes into the paper; second, continual smudging of the writing results, as the hand is still rubbing over the writing. He accordingly completes the 'hook', placing his hand right above the writing. This in turn is unsatisfactory though it is one adaptation which teachers permit left-handed children to acquire. It is difficult to achieve neat writing by this technique and since it is also a continual strain on the hand anyone adopting it will readily become fatigued if required to do much writing. Another method used by left-handers is to turn the paper sideways and write down towards the body, this being another attempt to acquire a comfortable position. Teachers are inclined to correct this position, but seldom suggest an acceptable alternative. One child pointed out as a neat writer though left-handed, was questioned as to his method of writing. It was found that he had no peculiar grip of the pen and a fairly free movement somewhat similar to that of a right-handed child. On inquiring how he avoided smudging his writing, it was found that he used blotting paper after every word. The product was neat but extremely slowly performed and with considerable unnecessary labour. Cole,[1] who made a study of the development of these habits, found that the three types illustrated in Figure 3 appeared frequently. Thus, these are not isolated cases, but are typical of left-hand writing positions.

[1] L Cole, *Psychology of the Elementary School Subjects*, New York: Farrar and Rinehart, Inc, 1934, pp 121-125

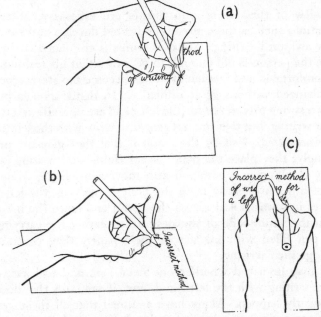

FIGURE 3 Illustration of Incorrect Writing Positions adopted by Left-Hand Writers: (*a*) arm hooked above writing; (*b*) writing in towards body; (*c*) with arm cramped in to side

CAUSES OF THE CHARACTERISTICS OF LEFT-HAND WRITERS

Not all of these characteristics are true of all left-hand writers, but they are typical of the writing and writing method of left-handed adults and children. Only by an analysis of the faults can one decide whether they are a necessary feature of writing with the left hand, when a transfer to right-hand writing might be the most satisfactory treatment, or whether they can be cured by a different technique of writing with the left hand in which case reform of the teaching is the solution.

All the faults listed above could easily be prevented by some guidance in the early stages. *Writing with the left hand is not the same as writing with the right, with only a change of hand.* For the movement to be the same with the left hand the writing would require to be performed from right to left, as only then would the hand be moving away from the body while progressing along the line of writing, as occurs with right-hand writing.

In view of this, some adjustments are necessary, otherwise situations such as these already indicated develop and result in slow awkward writing. What is worse is the fact that by the time the person is old enough to be aware that his technique is uncomfortable and inefficient, it has become too stereotyped to be changed without great difficulty. In many schools pupils with a strong preference for the left hand are now allowed to use it for writing, but they are not *taught* to write with the left hand, only *permitted*. Usually the result is that they grip the pencil wrongly; they place the paper as for right-hand writing inevitably resulting in a cramped arm movement, since, while the right arm moves away from the body in writing, the left arm moves in towards and across the body; and since the ink-well is on the wrong side of the desk necessitating the carrying of the pen filled with ink across their paper, they continually smudge their writing.

It may be asked whether one need look and feel awkward when writing with the left hand, and, if not, why that does so frequently happen. Many have assumed that all these symptoms are typical of what inevitably happens when one writes with the left hand. This is, in fact, one of the excuses given for the insistence on writing being performed with the right hand. It is now some years since investigators suggested that bad writing need not necessarily result from using the left hand and since constructive suggestions were made for the proper guidance of left-handers in learning to write. As early as 1927, West pointed out the need for a set of directions for dealing with the left-handed child.

There is a great deal of uncertainty among teachers as to what to do with the left-handed writer. Some proceed to make him over into a right-handed writer as expeditiously as possible. Others will do so only on condition that the child is below a certain age. Some will permit the child to write 'backhand' if it is natural for him to do so, others insist on the imitation of the formal slant. Definite and detailed recommendation is needed with regard to these and many other points bearing on the left-hand writer, the mirror-script writer, the subnormal, and the physically defective child. These pupils though in the minority, are often encountered, and the problems relative to their instruction are very confusing.[1]

[1] P V West, *Changing Practice in Handwriting Instruction*, Bloomington, Ill: Public School Publishing Co, 1927, pp 55-56

Cole, in 1934, in her book on the *Psychology of the Elementary School Subjects*, devoted considerable space to a discussion on the teaching of left-hand writers. As she pointed out:

If the left-handed child is independent enough to succeed literally single-handed in his contest with his teachers, some at least of whom will try to change him, his troubles have only just begun. All systems of writing are based on the assumption that the writer will use his right hand. The youthful and determined left-hander is usually forced into a system not in the least adapted to his needs.[1]

She then went on to state that the correct posture for the left hand is as comfortable and relaxed as that for the right. Orton,[2] in 1937, also discussed the correct position for the paper and the writing with the left hand; while Freeman[3] stated that the left-handed child is apt to acquire a highly awkward method of writing if left to himself, but if properly taught he may develop a habit of left-handed writing which is nearly as convenient as is right-hand writing. In 1939 Cole[4] discussed in great detail all the points of importance in teaching left-hand writing, and also explained how the peculiarities in left-hand writing arise in the present system which is quite unsuited to their needs. In 1945 an instruction manual was published by Gardner to serve as a guide both to teachers and to adults who had developed inefficient writing methods with the left hand. The writer's aim in the manual[5] is to assist left-handers to acquire an easy movement in writing, and by this means attain effortless, speedy writing. In the Editor's Foreword it is stated that it is the only manual which has been prepared specially for this purpose. The exercises are so planned that they can be used by the left-hander himself with a minimum of guidance.

These examples may suffice to show that material is available on teaching a left-handed child how to write; any suggestions which are now offered have thus at some time been given by

[1] Cole, *op cit*, p 122
[2] Orton, *op cit*, pp 179-185
[3] F N Freeman, *Solving Handwriting Needs As We See Them To-day*, Columbus, Ohio: Zaner-Bloser Co, pp 2-16
[4] L Cole, 'Instruction in Penmanship for the Left-handed Child', *Elementary School Journal*, vol XXXIX, 1939, pp 436-448
[5] W H Gardner, *Left Handed Writing—Instruction Manual*, Danville, Ill: The Interstate Co, 1945

others, though the emphasis may be slightly altered. They are assembled here and repeated in the hope that their inclusion in a book specifically on left-handedness may at last direct to the basic essentials the attention of those actually concerned with teaching writing and may result in a more positive attitude to the teaching of writing to left-handers. The suggestions may even instil a new spirit into the whole work of handwriting instruction, basing it on greater awareness of the differing abilities of individual pupils, and directing it more to the writing needs of later life.

SUGGESTIONS FOR THE TEACHING OF LEFT-HAND WRITERS

The following three improvements, if adopted and applied, would in themselves eliminate the awkward postures common in left-hand writers and make their writing movements smoother and less effortful.

I POSITION OF THE PAPER

Authorities on handwriting instruction have for many years been contending that the correct position of the paper when writing with the right hand is at an angle, with the left hand top corner of the paper nearer the body than the right. The reverse angle is correct when writing is performed with the left hand; in this case the effect of the wrong position is more unfortunate. If the paper is placed horizontally and directly in front of the person writing with the left hand several difficulties arise: (a) with the paper in the horizontal position a backward slope in the writing is easier, a regular forward slope being almost impossible; (b) as the hand progresses across the page the arm becomes more and more cramped in towards the body, whereas in right hand writing, which is moving away from the body all the time, the movement across the page becomes continually freer; (c) it is very difficult to see what has been written as the hand covers the words, which of course also leads to smudging of the paper. Accordingly, from the early writing lessons a left-handed child should sit slightly to the right side of the desk, with the paper placed alongside him on his left, thus allowing a freer arm movement. In this connection Gardner's manual gives the following instructions:

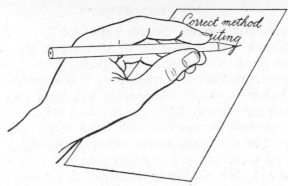

FIGURE 4   Illustration of Correct Position for Writing with
the Left Hand

Now study the position of your paper. At the left end of the first line of writing, your pencil will start far to the left. As you finish at the right edge of the paper, your pencil will still be slightly left of the mid-line. This is the reverse of the movement used by the right-handed writer who starts to the right of the mid-line of the body and writes far to the right.[1]

The paper should also be angled with the left-hand top corner higher than the right (as in Figure 4), the actual angle depending on the individual child and the slant of writing desired. If the paper is so placed, a freer movement develops; it eliminates the tendency to use the 'hook' movement, and it makes possible the development of vertical writing, or even a forward slant, without any strain. Many left-hand writers adopt this position of the paper themselves, but at the moment it is frequently done in face of the opposition of teachers who still insist on the central horizontal position of the paper.

II Type of Pen

The plain penholder with extra fine nib used in most school writing lessons was introduced at a time when the aim was slow meticulous writing of an elaborate type with fine up-strokes and heavier down-strokes. Hard as it is for a right-handed person to write with an extremely fine nib, it is almost impossible for the left-hand writer, as the push and pull movement with the left hand does not permit the efficient working of the nib. Fountain pens do not present the same difficulty, as they avoid

[1] *Ibid*, p 7

the necessity of carrying the nib full of ink across the page. This difficulty could, however, be overcome if the ink-wells could be fitted on either side of the desk. Even if the pupils are not permitted to use fountain pens, it is essential that left-handed children should use broader and more flexible nibs than their right-handed fellows so that they will not be slowed up unnecessarily or caused to jab holes in the paper when writing. The most suitable type of nib is one with a slightly turned-up point, or, in a fountain pen, one with a slightly bulbous end. It is possible to procure a nib cut with a reverse oblique point, which prevents the side being rubbed off the nib with continual use, a result that is apt to happen, especially with a fountain pen, where the nib is not changed frequently.

III GRIP OF THE PEN

It is necessary when writing with the left hand to grip the pen or pencil at least an inch or even an inch and a half from the point, in order to keep the hand below, and well clear of the stems of the letters, so that the child may be able to see what he is writing. This grip may also prevent him from smudging his writing, of which fear the right-handed child is free since his hand is usually alongside and to the right of the writing and consequently clear of it. A further precaution which is specially necessary with a left-handed child is to ensure that he does not grip the pencil or pen too tightly. This is a very common failing with all children when beginning to write; it causes tension and increases fatigue, but usually this grip is relaxed as the writing develops. Many left-handers, even adults, nevertheless clutch their pens in a vice-like grip and push hard in their attempts to write. Part of the explanation is again the fine hard nibs used in the early stages which will not work efficiently with the left hand, and frequently the ink will not come out at all, in which case the child tightens his grip and pushes harder. If, however, the nib is of such a type that it will work when guided across the page, without actual pressure having to be exerted down on the page, this difficulty will be overcome.

These three recommendations, on the position of the paper, the type of nib, and the grip of the pen, indicate the most important adjustments for the left-handed child, and they are also the simplest to apply. Various writers have stressed other points, for example, that the light should come over the right and not the left shoulder for the left-handed child so that his hand will not cast shadows on the writing. That is an adjustment, which, though desirable, would disturb the normal organisation of the class, and is only suggested as an additional, and not an essential, improvement. Cole and Gardner have both suggested that left-handed children should have their first writing practice at the blackboard since this encourages a full arm movement with greater freedom and a less cramped position. It also prevents the development of any such odd grips as the hook, since the hand is of necessity below the writing. *Frequent* practice of *large* writing on paper should be provided. It is inadvisable to make the child write very small letters in the early stages when his muscular co-ordination is not yet sufficiently developed for fine movements, as this results in tenseness and a tightening of the grip on the pencil. If the child is allowed to do big bold writing at the start, it will be found that as he develops better control, he reduces the size of the letters of his own accord. Economy was probably behind the insistence on small writing even in the early stages; with this went insistence on perfect formation of all the letters, which meant that only a line or two of writing was achieved in a writing period. As in many other skills, the character of the skill changes as the writing is speeded up; this implies that slow careful writing is not a training for speedy legible writing. Elaborate curls and twists on letters which can be achieved in slow writing are actually detrimental to legibility when the writing is speeded up; a simpler style would be easier to write and to read. Gardner's manual[1] for left-handers gives a series of exercises for developing this simple easy flowing writing at high speed without fatigue. These consist of groups of similar letters to be practised repeatedly. Cole mentioned similar exercises for the right hand, and suggested that they should be practised at greater and greater speed until they could be performed at a high speed with no decrease in legibility.

It is the object of these drills to establish rhythm, which is a highly

---

[1] *Op cit*, p 7

desirable element because it contributes to both speed and ease of writing. Other speed drills consist of writing a single sentence as many times on successive days as possible (without diminishing the legibility) in a short period of time—perhaps three minutes.[1]

In *The Backward Child* Burt pointed out:

I have seen teachers going round a class, showing other pupils how to place the paper and hold the pen, but leaving the left-hander to discover these things entirely for himself. Actually he needs more help, not less, if he is to learn how to manage his left hand efficiently. His paradoxical task is to produce with the left hand a style of writing evolved for the right. . . . There is, however, no necessity to describe in detail the requisite adjustments: they will be evident to the teacher after a little reflection, particularly if he first tries the experiment of left-handed writing himself.[2]

In view of the types of fault which are current among left-handers this policy of assuming that each teacher will know what to do and, what is more important, will do it, does not seem to be successful. As Cole stated in her article on the subject of teaching left-handers:

Because so few of them are found in any one place they will be trained in penmanship methods appropriate for right-handed children. Day after day throughout their first six school years, they will be taught by conscientious teachers to write badly. Six years from now most of them will emerge from elementary school using handwriting which is barely legible and which is produced awkwardly and at the cost of unreasonable effort. Teachers, parents and pupils will expect this situation; they do not know that these one hundred and fifty thousand pupils[3] will, under ordinary conditions, be merely the innocent victims of an inappropriate method of instruction.[4]

[1] L Cole, *Psychology of the Elementary School Subjects*, p 137
[2] Burt, *op cit*, p 340
[3] 150,000 pupils is Cole's estimate of the number of left-handers entering the first grade in American schools in any one year.
[4] L Cole, 'Instruction in Penmanship for the Left-handed Child', p 436

CHAPTER X

MIRROR-WRITING

DEFINITION OF MIRROR-WRITING

MIRROR-WRITING is the term used to describe writing which appears normal only when reflected in a mirror. The term usually refers to script in which the mirror-image is produced laterally—that is, the type in which all the letters and words are correctly formed in reverse and the whole proceeds from right to left, since other types are extremely rare. It has been found that some people have a peculiar facility for producing such writing spontaneously even without previous practice. The most famous of such persons was Leonardo da Vinci, whose notebooks were written in mirror-script. Another example is the 'Looking Glass Writing' illustrated in Figure 5, which Lewis Carroll used when writing to some of his young friends.

The inclusion of this phenomenon in a study of left-handedness is justified by the fact that almost without exception mirror-writing is produced either by left-handed persons or, at least, by use of the left hand. It has been established that Leonardo da Vinci drew with his left hand, and this can be verified from the manuscripts where it is clear that the lines and shading were performed with the left hand, as also was the mirror-writing, as may be seen in Figure 6 (facing p 94). Controversy has arisen as to whether da Vinci was natively left-handed or whether he only used his left hand as a result of paralysis of his right arm with which he was afflicted in later life. Contemporary writings indicate that he did in fact use his left hand even as early as the age of twenty. Lewis Carroll is known to have stammered, and it is suggested by Burt[1] that he may have been a changed left-hander.[2] The two examples cited

[1] Burt, *op cit*, pp 342-343
[2] It is easier to track down left-handers among artists than among writers, since, even when forced to use the right hand for writing, artists who have a strong left-preference will probably use their left hand for drawing and

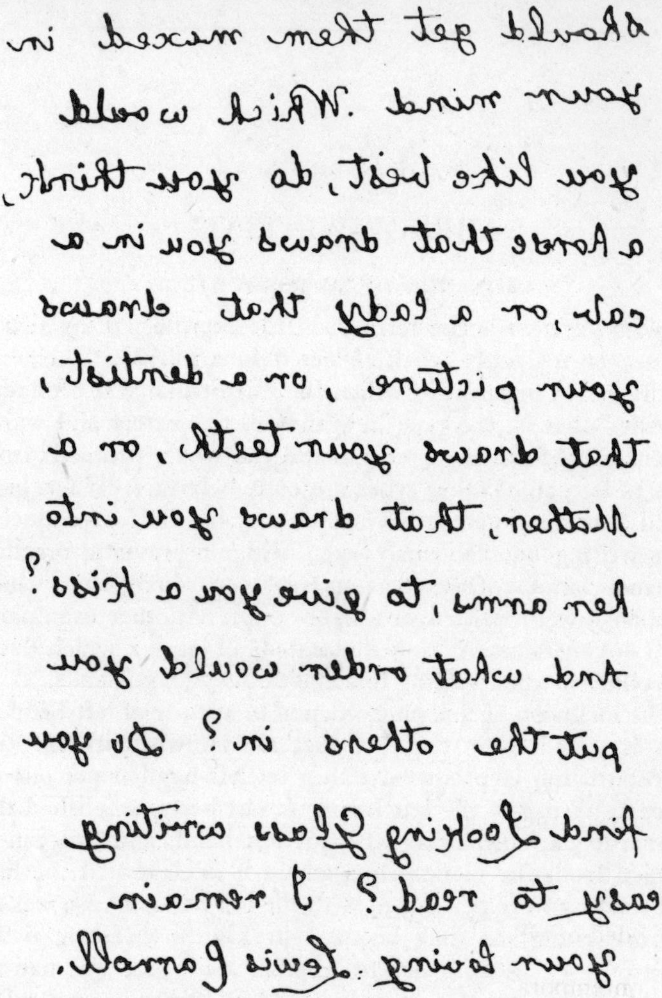
should get them mixed in your mind. Which would you like best, do you think, a horse that draws you in a cab, or a lady that draws your picture, or a dentist, that draws your teeth, or a Mother, that draws you into her arms, to give you a kiss? And what order would you put the others in? Do you find Looking-Glass writing easy to read? I remain your loving Lewis Carroll.

FIGURE 5 Extract from a Letter in Mirror-Writing by Lewis Carroll taken from *The Life and Letters of Lewis Carroll* by S D Collingwood

above reveal that mirror-writing may be found in highly intelligent persons. It has been shown by Gordon,[1] however, that its incidence is much higher among the mentally defective

painting. This may even be seen in children who, when forced to use the right hand for writing, still draw and even rule lines with the left.

[1] H Gordon, 'Left-handedness and Mirror-Writing, Especially among Defective Children', *Brain*, vol XLIII, 1921, pp 313-368

FIGURE 6   A Page from the 'Notebooks' of Leonardo da Vinci illustrating his use of Mirror-Writing

than in the normal population; while Fuller[1] has shown that it appears in certain personality disorders. Fragmentary mirror-writing even with the right hand is actually found in some children in the early stages of writing; this is understandable when one considers that there is nothing absolute about a left to right direction, and that in fact in some countries writing does actually proceed from right to left. Fluent mirror-writing is actually a left-hand production, for reasons which will be discussed later.

Mention of mirror-writing in individual patients is quite common in medical literature, but one of the few competent and comprehensive studies is that of Fuller,[2] who examined the different types of situation in which it appears spontaneously and the ways in which it can be artificially induced, and who also attempted to explain its occurrence. He pointed out that left-handed mirror-writing can be a symptom of

(a) physiological weakness through disease;

(b) weak-mindedness in children;

(c) left-handedness; or

(d) mere absent-mindedness in a normal person;

though, the more nervous a person is, the more likely he is to slip into mirror-writing. He also showed that it is a phenomenon which can be induced under hypnosis or under the influence of certain drugs, including alcohol, or by the attempt to write simultaneously with the two hands. He found, further, that there is a direct connection between the intellectual control and the amount of dissociation necessary to bring about the mirror-writing. Seeking some factor common to all these types of situation in which mirror-writing occurs spontaneously, or in which it can be artificially induced, Fuller concluded that the common basis is dissociation.

EXPLANATION OF MIRROR-WRITING

The most natural direction for movement with either hand is away from the body; the normal direction of our western writing is accordingly from left to right which is the natural

---

[1] J K Fuller, 'The Psychology and Physiology of Mirror-Writing', *University of California Publications in Psychology*, vol II, No 3, 1916, pp 199-265

[2] *Loc cit*

direction of movement with the right hand. In early times, in Greece for example, writing was for a time left to right then right to left on alternate lines, with the actual letters reversed in the right to left line. Some investigators have suggested that leftward writing, as for example in Hebrew and Arabic to-day, may be indicative of predominant left-handedness, but they have not considered the fact that it is only in our type of continuous, flowing writing, where the characters are joined, that one direction, namely the outward one, is favourable. For the left hand the movement away from the body, the easier movement, is from right to left; thus if there is no inhibiting factor, either visual or intellectual, or if this is temporarily removed, the left hand may produce mirror-script. It has been suggested that the transfer of training produced by teaching the right hand to do normal writing is towards mirror-writing with the left hand, at least in the absence of visual cues. Few left-handers have until recently been permitted to use their left hand for writing when at school, which would have impressed the left to right direction and inhibited mirror-script. Their spontaneous writing with the left hand, therefore, remains mirror-wise and is one explanation of the considerable facility with which some adults can produce mirror-writing. This facility will probably become less common in left-handers except among those who are forced to write with their right hand, since the practice in the left to right direction which the left hand will receive in producing the normal writing will inhibit it, while it will probably become more common among left-handed children in the early stages of learning to write. It is accordingly important that those in charge of children should be aware of the explanation and causes of mirror-writing so far as these are known, and that they should know how to prevent and treat cases which they do encounter.

Mirror-writing is not a sign of mental deficiency, though its prolonged occurrence is common in mental defectives. This is partly explained by the greater number of mental defectives who actually use the left hand for writing, and also by the absence of the factors which lead to its disappearance in a normal child. The realisation that he is actually producing a type of writing different from that produced by others, and unintelligible to them, is necessary in the left-hand writer before he will be prepared to change. Such a realisation will be dependent on a certain level of intelligence, perceptual ability and vision. In short, though an intelligent left-handed child may produce mirrored letters or words in the early stages more frequently than does a right-handed child, visual cues and comparison with the writing in books will lead to the realisation that his writing is in some way different, and will suggest a correction of the tendency; but such a realisation may not be present in a dull child. Probably if teachers were aware that a right to left direction in writing may be normal to a left-handed child and may be attempted by him, they could by suitable methods prevent the habit from developing. As individual schools and districts began to permit children to write with the left hand, the teachers were seldom aware of the difficulties, such as those mentioned in the preceding chapter, which might be encountered by the left-handed child. Another problem is this unconscious feeling for writing out from the body, which when encouraged with the right hand gives the correct direction, but with the left is incorrect. Lack of understanding of this may result in some teachers giving instructions or demonstrations which may encourage rather than prevent mirror-writing.

Spontaneous mirror-writing is not actually a very frequent occurrence in the normal child, though the potential ability to produce it is present in many left-handed adults, usually those who write with the right hand. The actual percentage of mirror-writers found in the school population has varied with the criterion adopted, since one may either ask the teachers to note all children who have ever produced mirror-writing, or note only those who produce it under experimental conditions. The figure given by Burt[1] is about one in five hundred children, while the figure quoted by Gordon[2] is 0·48 per cent in the ordinary elementary schools and 8 per cent in schools for mental defectives.

The most effective force in the prevention of mirror-writing is probably vision. Some children are evidently not aware that this type of writing in any way differs from the normal, since

[1] Burt, *op cit*, p 341
[2] Gordon, *op cit*, p 365

they can, in fact, read the product.[1] Others who produce mirror-writing are unable to read their product, but do not see that it is different because they are also unable to read ordinary writing, an inability which may be due to low intelligence or to a specific reading disability. The idea that all people can be classified into visiles, audiles and motiles, and that learning is predominantly or completely of one type has been abandoned in recent years, or at least the view that teaching should be directed through different sensory modes for different children. It does, nevertheless, remain true that certain individuals are more affected by, and employ, visual stimuli to a greater extent than other sensory stimuli, whereas others are more inclined to learn by touch. It is probable that mirror-writers are among the latter type, since the feel of the writing is correct in mirror-script. This suggestion was discussed in great detail by Burt:

> As the mirror-writer forms his letters, the correctness of the particular shapes and the wrongness of the general direction seem alike attributable to the fact that the nervous centres for motor control and the nervous centres for visual control may at times function in total independence. With nearly all of us, immediately an action becomes completely automatic, it tends to slip away from the control of the attentive eye, and to be left to the half-conscious guidance of the muscle-sense.[2]

With the guidance of the 'muscle sense' the result would be correct, provided the person were using the right hand, but when the hand used is the left, this reliance results in mirror-writing.

PREVENTION OF MIRROR-SCRIPT

Mirror-writing in the early stages does not present great difficulty, if handled correctly. The teacher should be aware that such a tendency may be potentially present in a left-handed child, particularly if he is more motor than visual in his learning. Mirror-script proceeds in a leftward direction, and can thus only be produced when the person commences at, or towards,

---

[1] Monroe has suggested that mirror-reading, that is, the ability to read mirror-script or tendency to read mirror-wise, may be connected with left-eyedness rather than left-handedness. M Monroe, *Children Who Cannot Read*, Chicago: University of Chicago Press, 1932, pp 87-88
[2] Burt, *op cit*, p 345

the right hand side of the page. To prevent such writing one must use some device to ensure that a potential mirror-writer always starts at the left of the page. This may be done by marking the starting place with a cross. If a child is nevertheless found to be producing mirror-writing thereafter, it may be necessary to stop all free writing for a time, and allow only slow careful writing from a copy until a rightward direction has been developed. Tracing over letters may also assist provided that the starting place is marked and that vision is emphasised as a further guide to the correct direction.

There is nothing normal about the one direction of writing and abnormal about the other. It should be remembered that in some countries it is the leftward direction which has to be cultivated. It is true, however, that some people have greater difficulty than others in accustoming themselves to the rightward direction of western writing. Mirror-writing does not necessarily have pathological significance, and its appearance in a left-handed child in the early stages of learning to write is not a matter of great concern, provided steps are taken to prevent it from becoming a habit. Only when it continues in an older child as his only, or usual, form of writing is it likely to be associated with mental deficiency. It most commonly accompanies left-handedness and nervousness or lack of attention, though the lack of attention may actually be concentration on some other aspect of the writing, speed for example. In conclusion, it is most important to remember that one should not regard, or appear to regard it as a sign of mental retardation. Parents and teachers who adopt this attitude are creating in the child an emotional 'set' and a feeling of nervousness, which is just the type of situation in which mirror-writing is produced unconsciously; while the emotional 'set' may even develop into hostility and result in a negative attitude to all school work.

CHAPTER XI

LATERALITY PREFERENCES AND READING DIFFICULTIES

THE realisation of the tendency discussed in the previous chapter for a right to left direction to be more natural with the left hand, combined with the frequency with which reversals occur in the reading of backward readers, has led investigators to consider the possibility that there may be some connection between laterality preferences and backwardness in reading. The studies carried out may best be considered under three main heads:

1 those suggesting a definite connection between left-handedness and reading disability;

2 studies of the effect of left-eyedness on reading;

3 studies of the effects of crossed laterality on reading.

In each of these three aspects some investigators have claimed to establish a connection between the two factors, while others have denied that any such connection exists. The discussion of these will be somewhat simplified if a selection of the findings is presented in antitheses as follows:

I LEFT-HANDEDNESS

For: Dearborn,[1] who claimed that one-third of 25 cases of backward readers were left-handed; Smith[2] who, when testing 50 backward readers and 50 normal readers, found a significant difference in their results with the Van Riper Critical Angle Board.

Against: Woody and Phillips,[3] on studying matched groups of

[1] Quoted by A I Gates, *The Improvement of Reading*, New York: The Macmillan Co, 1937, pp 342-343

[2] L C Smith, 'A Study of Laterality Characteristics of Retarded Readers and Reading Achievers'

[3] C Woody and A J Phillips, 'The Effects of Handedness on Reversals in Reading', *Journal of Educational Research*, vol XXVII, 1934, pp 651-662

136 pairs of right- and left-handed pupils, concluded that actual handedness had no effect on the type of reading responses made. The groups selected were deliberately chosen as representing pure types of left- or right-handedness.

II Left-Eyedness

For: Macmeeken[1] found a significantly higher percentage of left-eyedness in her retarded reading group of 140 children than is found in the normal population (58·6 and 37·28 per cent respectively), and she also found that the intelligence level of the left-eyed retarded reading children was significantly higher than that of the right-eyed children.

Against: Gates and Bond[2] found no significant difference in the numbers of any laterality type represented in two matched groups, one of 65 retarded readers and the other of 65 normal readers, and found no tendency for any particular type of eye-dominance or single eye superiority to be associated with any particular error.

III Crossed Laterality

For: Schonell[3] and Monroe[4] agreed in finding a higher incidence of mixed hand-eye dominance in backward readers than in normal pupils (Schonell 52 per cent, Monroe 45 per cent, normal 36 per cent).

Against: Witty and Kopel[5] studied 100 backward readers and 100 normal readers as a control group, and found no more reversals in the mixed dominant group than in the others.

For a detailed study of these various investigations the reader is referred to *The Improvement of Reading* by Gates.[6] The examples selected here from the mass of information and

---

[1] A M Macmeeken, *Developmental Aphasia in Educationally Retarded Children*, p 90

[2] A Gates and G L Bond, 'Relation of Handedness, Eye-Sighting and Acuity Dominance to Reading', *Journal of Educational Psychology*, vol XXVII, 1936, pp 450-456

[3] F J Schonell, *Backwardness in the Basic Subjects*, London: Oliver and Boyd, 1942, pp 162-169

[4] M Monroe, *Children Who Cannot Read*, pp 83-91

[5] P A Witty and D Kopel, 'Sinistral and Mixed Manual-Ocular Behaviour in Reading Disability'

[6] A I Gates, *The Improvement of Reading*, pp 342-352

numerous conflicting studies on aspects of laterality and their connection with language difficulty reveal that it would be impossible to state with any certainty the precise effect of left-preference generally on progress in learning to read. It is evident at least that the sole cause of backwardness in reading is not left-preference, though it seems possible that in some individuals, especially if it is combined with attempts to change the native preference, left-dominance may lead to confusion, and therefore to delay in acquiring a left to right approach in reading. As mentioned in connection with mirror-writing, there is nothing normal about one direction and abnormal about another. Other phenomena with which the child is familiar before he learns to read do not alter their identity when faced in the opposite direction or stood on their heads—a boy is still a boy in whatever direction he faces. Every child has, in fact, in learning to read, to learn to approach each word in a right-ward direction, and not in the manner of the interesting cases, cited by Gates,[1] who try a word from left to right and on failing to recognise it try again from right to left, and so on alternately, becoming more and more confused. A final point in this connection is the observation made by Fernald that whatever the effect of left-preference on reading:

The right-handed cases and the cases of matched eye-hand dominance resemble the cases in which the dominance is not matched, are as serious in their deficiency, learn by the same methods, and are as successful in the final outcome. The eye and hand dominance is not changed as a result of the remedial work; that is, the subject with unmatched eye and hand dominance learns to read and is able to read in an entirely normal manner with eye and hand dominance opposite.[2]

It may be that the investigators who have attempted to prove a connection between retarded reading and left-preference of some kind have for that reason tended to over-emphasise the place of reversals in the creation of bad reading. Frequent reversals do occur in reading at an early stage of learning, but they may reveal no more than that the backward reader is simply at that stage, in other words, they may be a symptom of

[1] Loc cit
[2] G R Fernald, Remedial Work in the Basic Skill Subjects, New York: The McGraw-Hill Book Co, 1943, p 150

a certain stage of reading not a cause of poor reading. An extreme example of this tendency to over-emphasise reversals is to be seen in the works of Orton and his followers. In his discussion of language difficulties, Orton[1] considered at great length what he called 'strephosymbolia' or the tendency to twist symbols; while Macmeeken[2] distinguished in her study between static and kinetic reversals. Though many criticisms have been made of Orton's theory, it does lead to some interesting observations on laterality which are worth considering. His explanation of the learning and recognition of words is based on what many maintained to be untenable neurological assumptions. It has been discussed earlier and will not be reconsidered here except in so far as it is of particular relevance to the problem of reading difficulty. Orton emphasised the importance of the early establishment of a dominant hemisphere, and claimed further that what he termed 'engrams' are formed in the associative tracts of both hemispheres, but that those in the non-dominant hemisphere are not usually employed. Should, however, clear-cut dominance not be established or should something interfere with its development, then this may result in a balance or indecision between the two hemispheres; and since the 'engrams' in the non-dominant hemisphere are mirror-wise, this may result in difficulty in recognising letters and words in their correct orientation. Without subscribing to Orton's theoretical assumptions it is possible to agree that confused laterality, either as a result of delay in acquiring dominant laterality, or of attempts to change hand preference, may result in poor orientation to words and therefore in backwardness in reading. Such a possibility is not ruled out by any of the studies to date, even such as have denied a connection between left-preference of hand or eye, or a connection between crossed laterality and retarded reading. It was suggested by Witty and Kopel,[3] for example, that though left-preference in general may not result in poor reading, unwise attempts to change handedness, or in some cases the presence of left-eye dominance, may result in right to left eye movements. They

[1] S T Orton, *Reading, Writing and Speech Problems in Children*
[2] A M Macmeeken, *Ocular Dominance in Relation to Developmental Aphasia*, London: University of London Press, 1939
[3] Witty and Kopel, *op cit*, p 131

accordingly suggest that it may be of value to employ speedy and reliable methods of determining hand and eye dominance in backward readers. In their investigation, Woody and Phillips[1] deliberately selected groups with 'pure' handedness preference, and concluded that left- or right-handedness *per se* is not a cause of reading difficulty. They did suggest the possibility, however, that different results might be obtained from groups of naturally left-handed pupils who had been trained to be right-handed, or from groups which had no really dominant hand. In this connection, Smith's[2] results on the Van Riper Critical Angle Board may be of some significance since that was the only test which did show a significant difference between the two groups of readers.

It is necessary to distinguish between the two types of study —first, those in which two groups have been constituted on the basis of success or failure on reading tests, with no regard to hand preference; and second, those where the groups have been arranged on the basis of hand preference. Since only a small percentage of the population actually use the left hand, and an even smaller one uses the left hand and left eye, caution must be observed in drawing conclusions from groups of the first type mentioned; while because of the small number of left-handers, few investigators have selected their groups on the basis of left- or right-hand preference. The best known study of the second type mentioned is that of Haefner.[3] Unfortunately, though he took great care in his selection of the two groups, he did, on the whole, confine his study to the less important aspects of the educational difference between left- and right-handers— for example, height, weight, strength, interests and play activity. In the study of school achievement which he did make, he found no reliable differences between the left-handed group and the other group, though he did find a tendency towards greater variability in school achievement, but not in intelligence, in the left-handed group.

It seems conclusive that neither left-handedness, left-eyedness, nor crossed laterality are in themselves important causes

[1] Woody and Phillips, *op cit*, p 662
[2] Smith, *op cit*, p 327
[3] R Haefner, *The Educational Significance of Left-handedness*, New York: Bureau of Publications, Teachers College, Columbia University, 1929

of backwardness in reading; nor do they appear to result in a greater number of reversals in children learning to read. It may be that differences in the methods of selection, such as those mentioned above, explain to some extent the differences in the results of the investigations on reading and laterality. Such contradictions reveal, however, the necessity for care in the selection of the groups, and in the methods of testing. The possibility cannot be ruled out that in individual cases left-preference, particularly if it develops an emotional disturbance, may act as a precipitating factor. Further, there is at least a distinct possibility that lack of dominance in hand or eye may lead to directional confusion and therefore to difficulty in recognition of words, unless some positive guidance is provided. In this connection, it may well be that finger-pointing, far from being a cause of bad reading as some teachers believe, actually arises from this insecurity in directional orientation. For this reason teachers giving instruction in the elements of reading should not assume, but should ensure, a consistent left to right approach not only to the actual printed line but also to each word. They would thereby reduce the incidence of backwardness in reading by removing a possible cause—directional confusion. Word methods of teaching to read, such as 'Look-and-Say', may tend to increase this confusion, unless supplemented by some technique which emphasises the importance of direction. Tracing of words in an attempt to become familiar with them, as suggested by Fernald[1] in her treatment of backward readers, or emphasis on the importance of the first letter in attempted recognition, as suggested by Gates,[2] which can be assisted by encouragement of the use of a dictionary, are but two possible ways of providing this sense of direction. The number of reversal errors made by children in learning to read, and particularly by backward readers, is probably influenced by the method employed in teaching reading much more than by any laterality characteristic of individual pupils.

[1] Fernald, *op cit*
[2] Gates, *op cit*

PART II

AN INVESTIGATION INTO THE LATERALITY CHARACTERISTICS OF A GROUP OF 330 CHILDREN

CHAPTER XII

THE THEORETICAL ASPECTS OF LATERALITY DISTRIBUTION IN THE NORMAL POPULATION

FREE operation of hand preference does not prevail in any community, even when the official policy of school authorities is claimed to be one of non-enforcement. Before and during his school days the child has a home environment where most adults with whom he comes into contact will attempt to enforce, or at least encourage, right-handedness, and the very nature of his environment, including the implements he uses, will direct him rightwards. Testing for hand preference is, moreover, made more difficult by the further complication that pressure towards conformity and right-handedness varies not only from community to community but also from one family to another. Thus, the strength of the initial tendency towards left-handedness determines only in part whether or to what extent the child will become left-handed. The attitude of parents to a child with left-handed tendencies is affected perhaps more than anything else by whether they or any close relatives happen also to be left-handed, by how they were treated in childhood, and by *their estimate* of the effect of such treatment. In a field where there are so few authoritative findings, and these frequently contradictory, personal experience counts for more than it otherwise would. It is, accordingly, improbable that two children with the same degree of initial hand-preference who had received even comparable treatment in their general environment of home or school could be found.

Awareness both that the appearance of left-handedness is affected by pressure towards right-handedness, and that the inequality of such pressure towards right-handedness in different children depends not on the strength of initial preference but on chance environmental factors, led the present writer to

consider that an analysis of left-hand preferences in a normal
unselected group would be an important topic of investigation,
though it is one which has not hitherto received much attention.
But before turning to the experimental details of this study it
may be well to give some consideration to the range of hand
preference to be anticipated in the normal population.

It would generally be admitted that in the normal population
the following range of tendencies exists: extreme right- and
left-handedness, ambidexterity or lack of preference, and slight
right- or left-handedness. Difference of opinion would, however, arise concerning the extent of each type. Some, like
Jackson[1] for example, would extend the range of indifference,
while others such as Brain[2] would consider ambidexterity or
indifference to be rare. Whatever one's initial preference or
tendency in infancy, the use and skill of one hand and not both
is generally perfected in man; further, in a right-handed society
the use of the right hand will be preferred to using the left.

What happens to those born 'not right-handed', that is, those
whose left hand is initially preferred even in a slight degree?

If the child is only slightly left-handed then the chances are
that he will become right-handed, since imitation, training and
the right-handed nature of everyday objects are all an induce-
ment to his adoption of the right hand.

An ambidextrous child, or to be more exact, one who has no
preference for either hand, will quickly appear to be right-
handed for similar reasons. This group consists of those who
are equally good with both hands, and would for that reason
have been able easily to adjust to left-handedness had society
required. There is also another group which has received little
consideration until recently. These are termed by Galen[3]
'ambilevous', that is, having two left hands, and included in this
group are those for whom it would be a matter of indifference
which hand they used, since they would be equally clumsy and
unskilful with either. These will also veer over gradually to
right-handedness.

Even without the employment of force to ensure right-

[1] J Jackson, *Ambidexterity*, London: Kegan Paul & Co Ltd, 1905
[2] R Brain, 'Speech and Handedness'
[3] Quoted in S T Orton, *Reading, Writing and Speech Problems in Children*

handedness the original distribution quickly becomes disturbed. In short, the left-handed group now contains only the more extreme left-handers, with, as suggested by Wile,[1] the possible addition of a few with a slightly less degree of preference but of too low mentality to make a complete transfer, and a few who for temperamental reasons 'prefer to be different', as did some of the patients referred to by Blau,[2] a finding which unfortunately led him to assume that left-handedness and negativism were necessarily connected. There is accordingly a general trend towards right-handedness. The variations in environmental pressure will, however, have the greatest effect on the borderline cases.

The more the problem is considered, the clearer it becomes that there is no obvious way of discerning the exact distribution of innate hand-preference. It is possible, at best, only to reason back from the observed preferences and attempt to allow for the effects of pressure, both direct and indirect; any test which claims to assess native hand preference should be viewed with suspicion.

From the preceding discussion it may be inferred that among the right-hand writers the following will appear, when considered in terms of initial hand preference:

(a) those naturally and extremely right-handed;

(b) those slightly right-handed;

(c) ambidextrous individuals, in the sense of having two skilful hands;

(d) those natively poor with both hands;

(e) any slightly left-handed;

(f) any strongly left-handed who have been either subjected to strong pressure or compulsion or who are of such a temperament that they find it preferable to conform to the majority rather than use the genuinely preferred hand.

The supposition that such a distribution is to be found among right-hand writers is the justification for a study of left-handedness which does not concentrate on those customarily termed left-handed.

---

[1] I S Wile, *Handedness: Right and Left*, Boston: Lothrop Lee and Shepard, 1934

[2] A Blau, *The Master Hand*

CHAPTER XIII

AIMS OF THE STUDY AND SELECTION OF THE GROUP FOR INVESTIGATION

THE PROBLEM

THE investigation to be reported was undertaken with the aim of making an analysis of the type and degree of laterality characteristics to be found in the normal population, and of instituting a comparison of the nature and degree of different laterality characteristics in any one individual. The initial problem was to study the range and amount of different types of handedness, eyedness, earedness and footedness as they actually appear in a normal group, and to make a comparison of these in different children. The discussion in the previous chapter indicated the range of hand preference anticipated in an unselected group of right-hand writers, while it was hoped in addition to obtain, incidentally during the testing periods, a considerable amount of qualitative data on many of the aspects which affect a child's hand preferences, on pressures toward right-handedness, on the children's own attitudes to left-handedness and on left-handedness among their relatives. The investigator's own use of the left hand would, it was hoped, help to create an atmosphere for such confidences, especially among those who had some reason to anticipate the disapproval of society for their left tendencies. In many instances the subjects noticed the author's use of the left hand in writing, but if they did not, sometimes an admission that she used that hand helped with certain children. Information on the educational attainments and intelligence of the subjects would, it was hoped, throw some light on the important problem of the effect of laterality preferences on educational achievement, or at least indicate lines for a further study.

SELECTION OF THE EXPERIMENTAL GROUP

Three related aspects had to be considered in establishing the experimental group, the composition and size of the group, and the method of testing. The use of an unselected group as far as hand preference was concerned though it would result in relatively few left-hand writers was, it was felt, likely to yield many interesting degrees of left-hand preference in the right-hand writers, while this policy was also necessitated by the desire to make a comparison of hand preferences with other laterality preferences, for example, eyedness and footedness. The nature of the testing and the size of the group were obviously closely connected, since it would be possible either to test a large group with a few tests or with a questionnaire, or a relatively smaller group with a more complete battery of tests. The latter method was decided upon in view of the research on the reliability and validity of questionnaires,[1] and because the aims of the study seemed to be better served by such a method, since it would yield more qualitative material than could possibly be secured if each child were tested for only a short time.

The complete Primary VII class in eight Glasgow schools was used for the study, which gave an experimental group of 330 children (162 boys and 168 girls), with an age range of 11-12 years of age. The following points were considered in making the selection:

1 *Children* were selected as subjects because the educational significance of the problem is an important aspect, and because the attitude to left-handedness has altered so much in recent years that relatively few adults write with the left hand. For that reason it was considered important to study the distribution under present conditions when the official policy is to permit left-hand writing.

2 *Both sexes* were included and it was considered important (*a*) that they should be in approximately equal numbers since a sex difference in handedness had been found by previous investigators, and (*b*) that they should be in the same class, so that their school conditions at least could be comparable.

3 *Complete classes* in the various schools selected were con-

---

[1] *Supra*, pp 53-4

sidered the most suitable units from which to constitute the group, in order to make the conditions of learning as comparable for the group as possible, an important consideration in a study such as this.

4 *The Primary VII class* in the Primary School was thought to be most suitable for the testing for the following reasons:

(*a*) At that stage the children are still, in Scotland, unselected as far as ability is concerned (except for those with I Q under 70 who may have been sent to a Special School). This is the highest class of the primary school before selection for secondary education takes place.

(*b*) It was possible at that stage to find classes containing both boys and girls being taught together.

(*c*) The children at that stage had been at school long enough to be affected by the school attitude to left-handedness.

(*d*) At that stage it would be easier to test with a comprehensive battery of tests; with younger children it would be difficult to make the duller members of the group comprehend the instructions.

(*e*) Children in that class had been long enough at school— seven years—for it to be particularly valuable to consider their educational achievement, since they had in fact completed a stage of their school career.

(*f*) Their presence in that class meant that it was possible to supplement the test results with their intelligence and achievement scores, information which had been gathered by the authorities in connection with the promotion of these children to secondary school courses.

5 *Glasgow* was the district selected for the investigation. Since it was clear that it was impossible for one investigator unaided to make an intensive study of the type planned and also cover a sufficient sample of the population of Scotland to make generalisations for the whole country, it seemed wiser to limit the study to one area, for which Glasgow seemed admirably suited, because of its size and of the wide range of home backgrounds represented in the schools.

The Director of Education agreed that the testing might take place in a selected number of schools. A selection of schools was then made, and in order to have as representative a group as possible, it was decided to include schools classed by the authorities as above average, average, and below average, in the ratio 1:2:1. Since all children in Primary VII of the schools selected were to be tested, this grading of the schools was only an approximate one, and the estimate of the authorities was used as the guide in the rough grading. In practice this method worked very well and yielded a fairly well-defined pattern of below average, average, and above average distribution of the selected schools, this in spite of the fact that no deliberate selection of pupils does take place for entrance to most public schools at this level, except possibly that made as a result of the district in which the school is situated. In order to represent the large Roman Catholic population in Glasgow, the children of which attend 'transferred' schools, and which therefore constitutes something in the nature of a selection, two of the eight schools being used for testing were Roman Catholic.

One complete class, Primary VII, was tested in each of the eight primary schools. No difficulty was encountered in obtaining parallel groups in each of the schools, since most had only one such class at the Qualifying Stage, while in one instance where there were three classes at that stage, one contained girls, one boys only, and the third was a mixed class; the mixed class was accordingly the one used for testing to keep it comparable with those in the other schools. For details of the numbers tested in each school and in each grade of school see Table I.

TABLE I

NUMBER OF CHILDREN TESTED BY SCHOOLS[1]

School	Number of Subjects		
	Boys	Girls	Total
A1	20	21	41
A2	22	25	47
B1	20	19	39
B2	23	25	48
B3	21	18	39
B4	21	19	40
C1	19	19	38
C2	16	22	38
Totals	162	168	330

[1] Above average A1, A2; Average B1, 2, 3, 4; Below Average C1, C2

CHAPTER XIV

SELECTION OF TESTS AND METHOD OF TESTING

SELECTION OF TESTS

SINCE the aim of the study was to make a comparison of the various aspects of laterality preferences, in particular those of hand, foot, eye and ear, a battery of tests had to be designed which would assess all these aspects as effectively as possible. In the series of tests of handedness, which was more extensive than that of the other aspects, each test was selected to measure a particular aspect of hand dominance. All the tests used were adapted both to meet the aims of the study and to suit the age of the children tested.

I HANDEDNESS

The hand used for writing had clearly to be ascertained, which was done by questioning the subject, whose statement was checked in the course of the testing when he was required on several occasions to write his name on test papers. The tests can be divided into those which determined the child's *preference* for the right or left hand in various selected tasks, and those which measured his *relative ability* with right and left hand. Three tests of the former type were employed, giving a measure of the hand preferred in throwing, in reaching, and in screwing and unscrewing. 'Throwing' was an obvious choice since it is an activity in which a child frequently indulges and in which he acquires a considerable degree of skill, making him, for that reason, acquire a definite preference for one hand or other, frequently, though not always, that used in writing. Most previous investigators have noted the 'throwing' hand either by means of a questionnaire or in the form of a test, and have found it to correlate highly with the hand used in writing. The existence of any discrepancy between the hand used in an acquired, skilled task such as throwing and the hand used in writing, would suggest that the former tests were revealing left-handedness in persons who had been encouraged or forced to use the right hand for writing. Various investigators have claimed that the arm used in reaching is on the same side as the dominant hand. Certainly if an object is directly in front of a person he does usually reach for it with a particular hand; while even in instances where it would be more effective to reach with the other, many persons still use the 'preferred' hand. 'Screwing' is another activity for which, though it requires strength rather than skill, most people do consistently prefer one hand. Though relative strength of the two hands, as measured for example by a hand-dynamometer, seems to have little connection with the dominant hand in other respects, as shown by Whipple[1] and Burt,[2] and was for that reason omitted from this battery, it was felt that the preferred hand for screwing would be worth noting. One test, in which speed was compared, measuring relative ability of the two hands was employed. It was designed to be fairly close to the movements involved in ordinary writing, to ascertain how far the untrained hand was below the trained with regard to speed. Obviously in the extremely right- or left-handed the margin would be great, whereas when scores were relatively alike in spite of the training received by the writing-hand the inference would be either that there had been comparable potential skill in the two hands or that the untrained hand would have been superior had it received the training. The Van Riper Critical Angle Board[3] was included in the investigation to test the test rather than to study the children. The test of simultaneous writing which was also included was a somewhat simplified version of the Van Riper Test, but similar to it in principle in that the hand which reverted to mirror-writing under the testing conditions was regarded as the non-dominant hand. Two other tests were included which do not fall exactly into either of the above-mentioned categories. One was a test of 'fine' movement, where, though the performances were timed, it was in fact the skill of the two hands which was

---

[1] Whipple, *op cit*, pp 100-109
[2] C Burt, *op cit*, pp 271-272
[3] *Supra*, pp 59-62 for discussion of the test

actually being observed. The remaining test was one of alternating movement, and was included in the battery because of suggestions that the dominant hand has greater facility in actions quite divorced from skill. In this test the relative ability of the two hands to maintain a simultaneous alternating movement of the wrists was observed.

II FOOTEDNESS

Some investigators have claimed a high correlation between footedness and handedness, while others have maintained that the correlation is low. The studies of Cuff[1] and Haefner[2] are examples of that disagreement, since Cuff found that all his subjects who were right-handed were also right-footed, while Haefner reported that only a few of his subjects showed foot dominance, and that the coefficients between hand and foot tests were likely to be low. It appears that the findings depend on whether one or several measures are employed in measuring footedness. In short, when the only criterion was the foot used in kicking, the correlation appears to have been high, while on a battery of tests it seemed to be low. To examine this divergence the foot used in kicking was observed in this battery, and two other tests were included, the foot used in hopping, and the foot used in stepping off. Thus the tests of footedness were directly comparable with each other since they were all measures of preference for one foot or the other.

III EAREDNESS

Though batteries of tests of laterality usually include eyedness, they have rarely contained any tests of earedness. In view of the definite preferences shown by persons when, for example, answering the telephone, it was considered worth including two tests of earedness to discover how closely the choice in that corresponded with the dominant hand. Two tests were accordingly designed, in one of which the object was actually held to the ear to give the dominant hand its maximum play, whereas, in the other test, the ear had to be placed down to the object

[1] N B Cuff, 'A Study of Eyedness and Handedness'
[2] Quoted by J E Downey, 'Laterality of Function'

which was not touched with the hands. A third test which it was thought might have some connection with the preferred ear was tentatively included in this group and was designed to measure the direction in which the head was turned as a result of a sound coming from behind but equi-distant from the two ears. All the tests included in this group were, it should be stressed, tests of preference and not of aural acuity.

IV EYEDNESS

In view of the study made by Crider[1] of tests of eye dominance it seemed necessary to select tests of eyedness with special care. Previous investigators found, however, that simpler tests have as good results as the more complicated and elaborate; and for that reason, after considering the earlier studies, it was decided to select four of the simpler tests of eye dominance and include them in the battery. Two of the tests were of the type which required a deliberate choice of one eye only; while the other two ascertained the sighting eye when both were actually open.[2] The four tests selected made it possible to study the consistency of use of one eye in a particular test; to compare the eye used in two very similar tests, to see whether this was still consistent for two types of eyedness; and finally to compare the results of these tests with the results obtained on the tests of other aspects of laterality preference.

In Table II are listed the various tests used and the order of applying the tests to each child.

METHOD OF TESTING

The testing was so arranged that one group of schools was tested, that is, one above average, two average, and one below average; then the second group was tested, making a total of eight schools. This precaution was taken to make certain that any slight changes resulting from practice gained in testing should not influence any particular grade of school. Each child in a class was tested individually, boy and girl alter-

[1] B Crider, 'Unilateral Sighting Preference' No 2, 1935, pp 163-164. (*Supra*, pp 67-8 for discussion of significance of this.)
[2] *Supra*, Chapter VII for a detailed discussion of the different types of eyedness

TABLE II

Tests Used and Order of Applying[1]

Laterality Characteristic	Name of Test	Order of Applying	Total Numbers of Tests
Handedness:			8
	Screwing	1	
	Reaching	12	
	Throwing	18	
	Fine Movement	14	
	Speed of Crossing	9	
	Simultaneous Writing	4	
	Van Riper Test	6	
	Alternating Movement	16	
Footedness:			3
	Kicking	5	
	Stepping	8	
	Hopping	17	
Earedness:			3
	Sound in Box	11	
	Stop Watch	15	
	Head Turning	3	
Eyedness:			4
	Cone Test	7	
	Hole in Card	13	
	Peep Show	2	
	Cylinder	10	
Total			18

nately, and the testing was more or less in alphabetical order, with the exception of absentees who had to be left until the end. In some instances it was necessary to return to the school to test absentees, but it seemed important to do this, as the aim was to include complete classes. Information was sought from each child on the number of siblings, their age and their handedness, and on any other left-handed relatives. The presence of any twins in the families was also noted. If a child wrote with his left hand, or had ever done so, additional questions were asked on difficulties he might have encountered, and on attempts to change his handedness. Any other details thought to be of value were also noted. The actual time required to test and question each child was approximately thirty minutes.

[1] *Infra*, for details of the tests

A writing test was also given to each class at some time during the two weeks. The Paul West Test[1] was selected as the most suitable because it was claimed to measure both speed and quality of writing. As it was impossible to wait until the complete class was present to give the test, it was given when there were the fewest absentees; these had later to be given the test under comparable conditions, either in a group or individually.

DETAILS OF TESTS

Before any discussion of the results can be understood it is necessary to be familiar with the exact details of the method of carrying out the testing. In tests which measured preference the child was given four attempts. Since that was a sufficient number to disclose inconsistencies in choice, a greater number of trials would not have been more significant. Harris[2] found that three trials were sufficient. Details of the tests and of the instructions to the children are presented here in the order in which they were given to the subjects, not grouped according to the laterality characteristic they were designed to measure. Several considerations had to be borne in mind when deciding the order of the tests and the phrasing of the instructions. It was important that similar tests of a particular aspect should be separated as far as possible so that the results of one should not affect the other. Since left-handedness is greatly influenced by the disapproval of society it was necessary to design the tests so that the child was not aware of what was being investigated. Each test had accordingly some other apparent motive in order to prevent the child becoming aware of what was being studied so that his genuine preferences would be ascertained and not others displayed in the hope of pleasing the investigator—a precaution also stressed by other investigators. For the same reason, each aspect was tested instead of merely taking the child's word. Finally, in a battery containing as many as eighteen tests it was important that the tests should be so designed that they would retain the children's interest. They

[1] P V West, *Manual for The American Handwriting Scale*, New York: The A N Palmer Co, 1929

[2] A J Harris, *Harris Tests of Lateral Dominance*: Manual of Directions for Administration and Interpretaton, New York: The Psychological Corporation, 1947

were planned and worded to suit children of about twelve years of age, and would therefore require to be adjusted and reworded for younger or older children.

Test 1 *Screwing* (Handedness)

For this test a small screw-top bottle, filled with coloured counters, was used. The test consisted of screwing and un-screwing the top of the bottle, and of arranging the counters.

The child was seated at a table, and instructed to place his hands behind his back. When in that position, the bottle was placed directly in front of him, equidistant from each hand.

Instructions: When I say 'Go', take the top off the bottle, clap your hands once, then put the top back on the bottle, as quickly as you can. Ready—Go.

Put your hands behind your back again. This time, when I say 'Go', take the top off the bottle, empty out the counters, then arrange them in piles, a separate pile for each colour, as quickly as you can. Ready—Go.

Now put the counters back in the bottle, and screw on the top.

Though speed was deliberately emphasised, the test was in reality one of hand preference, and not of relative speed. The hand used at each trial, to remove and to replace the top, was noted, and also details of the method of arranging the counters, whether with one hand, or both. This test yielded quantitative results from the number of times each hand was used for screwing; but the methods of arranging the counters were so variable that they could only be recorded verbally. Though the results of the second part of this test were vague they were of some interest with particular pupils.

Test 2 *Peep Show* (Eyedness)

The test involved looking through a small hole into a box, which made it necessary for the child to make the choice of one eye. A circular hole, half an inch in diameter, was cut in the front of a small cardboard box. Half an inch was also cut off the back of the lid to allow light to enter the box, and so that printed cards could be slipped down inside facing the hole. Four white cards, each bearing a printed word, were cut to fit the space at the back of the box.

The child was seated with his hands behind his back. The box with a card in place was held a short distance from his eyes with the hole towards him at eye level and equidistant from each eye.

Instructions: Put your eye up to the little hole and see if you can tell me what is written on the card inside the box.
What is on this one?

The test was given four times with a different card each time. The instructions were worded to imply that the task was to read the word, while the result noted was the eye put to the hole at each trial.

Test 3 *Head Turning* (Earedness)

This test involved turning of the head at a sound made directly behind the subject. The child was seated at the table, looking straight ahead, and with his hands behind his back. The experimenter stood directly behind the child, making certain that he was sitting straight.

Instructions: I am going to make a sound with a pencil just behind your head. Whenever you hear it, turn your head. Are you listening?

This test was repeated three more times and the child was encouraged to turn more quickly each time. Speed was again emphasised in this test, and at the fourth trial, the sound was then delayed a few seconds, which sometimes resulted in the child anticipating it, and made him realise that attention was being paid to whether or not he listened for the sound. The result noted was the side to which he turned his head at each of the four trials.

Test 4 *Simultaneous Writing* (Handedness)

This test consisted of writing numbers with both hands at the same time. The child was seated at the table with a quarto sheet of plain paper in front of him and a pencil in each hand.

Instructions: You are going to write with both hands at the same time. You are going to write a figure '2' with each hand, side by side and at the same time. Below that write a '3' with both hands, then '4' and so on, as I say the numbers up to '9', but we'll miss out '8'. Just to make it really difficult, you must shut your eyes while doing it. Ready—2, 3, 4, 5, 6, 7, 9.

Now that you know exactly what to do we will try once more on the other side of the paper, and a little quicker this time.

As this task gives most people a great deal of trouble, it seemed better to assure the child that one was aware of the difficulty. A note was made of the number of times either hand drew a mirror-image instead of the correct one. This was noted separately for each attempt, and details were also taken of the figures which were mirrored.

Test 5 *Kicking* (Footedness)

This test was to determine which foot the child used in kicking. He was placed at a distance of several feet from a chair, then given a ball of paper.

Instructions: You are going to try and kick the ball of paper between the legs of that chair. You will have four turns. See how many times you can kick it right through.

Accuracy was emphasised here to give purpose to the test from the child's point of view, and to ensure that he would kick with the foot he was in the habit of using. A note was made of the foot used in kicking at each of the four attempts.

Test 6 *The Van Riper Test* (Handedness)

The task in this test was to copy a diagram correctly with both hands at the same time and on opposite sides of a vertical board.

The Van Riper Laterality Apparatus or Critical Angle Board[1] was used. Essentially this consists of two vertical boards on a horizontal base, so arranged that each vertical board can be rotated from a position parallel to the chest through 90 degrees, until the boards are back to back. Paper is arranged on these boards so that a record may be kept of the drawings with each hand. The paper is unwound from one roller and on to the other as the test proceeds. Thus, finally, the left-hand drawings for all subjects are on one side of the paper, and the right-hand drawings on the other. The apparatus was somewhat adapted for the present study to make it portable. The horizontal base was made to hinge in two places, so that it would fold up and

---

[1] C Van Riper, 'The Quantitative Measurement of Laterality'

protect the rollers, and a cover was made for the top. This did not, however, alter the apparatus in any essentials.[1]

The child was seated with the apparatus on the table in front of him. The vertical boards were set at zero degrees, or parallel to the chest. A diagram was placed on the wall some feet away, and about 30 degrees above eye-level. The child was then given a pencil in each hand.

Instructions: I want you to try and copy that drawing with both hands at the same time. Do it with the left hand on here (indicating the left vertical board), and with the right hand on here, (indicating the right vertical board). You must keep looking at the drawing, follow it with your eyes, don't look down at your hands. Put the pencils ready on the paper. Ready—Go.

At the first attempt the child was permitted to draw at his own speed, but when he had grasped the procedure he was made to draw more quickly, and after beginning the diagram, was not allowed to pause until it was completed. Next, each vertical board was moved back through 30 degrees, and the paper turned to a new part. The child was again instructed to draw the diagram with both hands at the same time. This was repeated with the boards at sixty and ninety degrees.

The test was next carried out with the boards at the same four angles, but instead of asking the child to copy a visual pattern, he was instructed:

When I say the number '3', I want you to draw a '3' with both hands at the same time. Have your pencils ready on the paper. Shut your eyes. Ready—3.

The test was also carried out with a third and fourth diagram, which were both patterns, the fourth being the reverse of the third. For illustrations of the diagrams used in the testing, see Figure 7.

The results noted were, for each diagram, the hand which drew a reversed or mirror-image of the diagram, and the angles at which this happened.

Test 7 *Cone Test* (Eyedness)

This test involved looking through a cone-shaped object, apparently using both eyes, but the situation was such that only

[1] *Supra*, pp 59-62 for a more detailed study of the apparatus and illustration clarifying the explanation

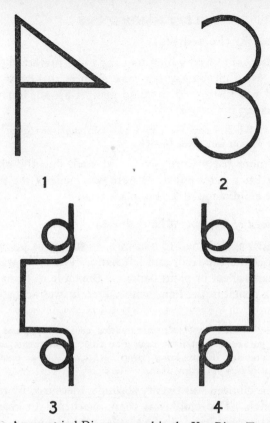

FIGURE 7   Asymmetrical Diagrams used in the Van Riper Test: Diagrams
1, 3 and 4 were shown to the child; while for Diagram 2 the word
'three' was given orally to be reproduced as a figure

one eye could actually be used. A cardboard cone, about eight
inches in length, was used. It was wide enough at one end to go
over both eyes, and tapered to about an inch at the other end.
The child stood several feet from the investigator, and held the
cone in both hands.

Instructions: When I say 'Go', hold up the cone, putting it over both
eyes. Look through it with both eyes, and tell me how many fingers
I am holding up. Ready—Go. How many fingers?

This was repeated three more times, and the eye which was
visible through the narrow end of the cone at each trial was
noted as the sighting eye. It may be seen from Figure 2 how
this test looks to the experimenter.[1]

[1] *Supra*, facing p 60

Test 8 *Stepping* (Footedness)

This test was to find which foot the child preferred to use in stepping, when circumstances were such as to favour neither. The child was instructed to stand against a wall, but with his heels touching it.

Instructions: When I say 'Go', take two big steps out from the wall. Step as far as you can. Ready—Go.

Three more trials were given. At each one the child was encouraged to greater effort. A note was made of the foot with which the child stepped first at each trial.

Test 9 *Speed of Crossing* (Handedness)

This test was designed to measure, as simply as possible, the relative speed of the right and left hand. The child was seated with a quarto sheet of plain paper on the table in front of him, and with a pencil in the hand with which he was accustomed to write.

Instructions: When I say 'Go', start making crosses along the paper as quickly as you can. Just little ones like this (indicating thus X). If you finish one line before I say 'Stop', start another at once. Make them as quickly as you can. Ready—Go.

The time allowed was twenty seconds, measured by means of a stop watch. The child was then instructed to change the pencil to the other hand, and a similar trial was given with that hand. The test was then repeated with each hand. The results noted were the number of 'crosses' made with each hand at the first and second trials, and the total number of crosses with each hand.

Test 10 *Cylinder* (Eyedness)

This test indicated which eye was preferred when only one might be used, but differed from Test 2, in that the cylinder was actually held to the eye.

The apparatus consisted of a cardboard cylinder twelve inches in length and one inch in diameter. The child was handed the cylinder, then told to stand at a distance of several feet.

Instructions: Take that tube in both hands. When I say 'Go', put it up to your eyes, and look through it. Tell me the colour of the counter I will hold up. Ready—Go.

This was repeated three more times, and a note made of the eye to which the cylinder was placed at each of the four trials.

The emphasis placed on speed, together with the fact that he was expected to name colours, directed the child's attention away from the actual placing of the cylinder to his eye, and thus indicated his natural preference.

Test 11 *Sound in Box* (Earedness)

This test indicated which ear was preferred when a choice had to be made. The child was seated at the table with his hands behind his back. A stop watch which was ticking was placed in a box, and laid on the table directly in front of him.

Instructions: Tell me if that watch is ticking. You may put your ear down to it if you wish, but do not touch it with your hands. Is it ticking? (or: Can you hear it ticking?)

This was repeated three more times, twice with the watch stopped, and once when it was ticking. The result noted was the ear placed to the watch at each trial.

Test 12 *Reaching* (Handedness)

This test revealed which hand, or rather, which arm, was used in energetic reaching. The child was seated at a table with his hands behind his back. The investigator stood directly behind him, holding a cylinder above the child's head, almost out of reach, but in an equally favourable position for either hand.

Instructions: When I say 'Go', reach up with one hand, and try to touch this tube. Ready—Go.

This test was repeated three more times, and for each trial the cylinder was held slightly higher than for the preceding one. A note was made of the arm used for reaching at each of the four trials.

Test 13 *Hole in Card* (Eyedness)

This test showed the eye used in sighting when both were open, but only one could be used. Thus it was similar to Test 7, but a different apparatus was used. The child stood at a dis-

K

tance of several feet, facing the experimenter. He was given a piece of cardboard, eight inches by eleven, with a half-inch hole in the centre.

Instructions: When I say 'Go', take the card in both hands and hold it up in front of your eyes so that you can see through the little hole. Stretch out your arms in front of you, and look with both eyes. Ready —Go. Tell me how many fingers I am holding up.

This was repeated three more times, and a note made of the eye which could be seen through the hole at each of the four trials.

Test 14 *Fine Movement* (Handedness)

This test was an attempt to measure the relative speed and accuracy of the left and right hand. Small silver beads, three-sixteenths of an inch in diameter; a narrow glass tube; small tweezers and a stop watch were used. The child was seated with the box of beads, the tweezers and the glass tube in front of him.

Instructions: I want to find out how quickly you can put five of these little beads into the tube. Pick them up with these (indicating the tweezers), one at a time. Ready—Go.

This test was repeated with the other hand. A note was made of the hand used first, the time taken with each hand, and any undue clumsiness with either hand.

Test 15 *Stop Watch* (Earedness)

This test was to determine which was the preferred ear in a situation where a choice had to be made, but differed from Test 11 in that there the child was not permitted to touch the watch, while here it was actually held in the hand. This was to discover the influence of the dominant hand on the choice. The child was seated with his hands behind his back, and a watch on the table in front of him. The watch was placed at an equal distance from each hand.

Instructions: When I say 'Go', pick up the watch with one hand, hold it to your ear, and count how many ticks you can hear before I say 'Stop'. Ready—Go ... (about fifteen seconds later) Stop. How many did you hear?

This test was repeated three times. Before each trial the

watch was replaced in such a way that it favoured neither hand, and the child was instructed to start with his hands behind his back. A note was made of the ear to which the watch was placed at each of the four trials, and also of the hand used to lift the watch.

Test 16 *Alternating Movement* (Handedness)

This was a test of the relative ability of the left and right hand to carry out simultaneous rapid alternating movements. The child was seated with his arms in a bent position. A demonstration was given, the hands being rotated rapidly in opposite directions, with movement from the wrists.

Instructions: See for how long you can make both your hands move like this. Make them go opposite ways, as quickly as you can. Go on until I tell you to stop. Ready—Go.

Usually within a very short time one of the hands ceased to make the correct movement. The test was continued until some difference such as that was observed. A note was made of the relative ability of the two hands at the start and, where one tired more quickly, that was also noted. In one or two instances, the child found it impossible even to make both hands perform the task simultaneously.

Test 17 *Hopping* (Footedness)

Here the foot preferred for hopping was tested. The child stood with his back to the wall and his feet together.

Instructions: When I say 'Go', you will start hopping towards the end of the room. See how far you can get before I say 'Stop'.
Ready—Go . . . Stop.

At each trial the time allowed was reduced and the child encouraged to attain greater speed. A note was made of the foot selected for hopping at each of four trials.

Test 18 *Throwing* (Handedness)

This test was to discover which hand the child selected when throwing. A small box was placed on a chair, and the child stood at several feet distance, holding a paper ball.

Instructions: Try and throw that ball into the box. You will have four chances, see how many times you can get it in the box.

No mention was made of the hand to be used, and after each attempt the ball was thrown back to the child who selected which hand he would use. When four trials had been made with the selected hand, the child was then given one trial with the non-preferred hand. A note was made of the hand selected, and also of his relative ability in throwing with the non-preferred hand.

WRITING TEST

In addition to the battery of eighteen tests of laterality characteristics just described, a writing test was given to all the subjects. After studying the various available writing tests it was decided that the American Handwriting Scale, full details of which are to be found in the manual,[1] was the most suitable for the purpose of this investigation, since it was designed to measure quality and speed of writing and there were no such writing scales standardised on Scottish children. It seemed worth experimenting with this test in the absence of a better, since even if the quality scale provided with the test were found not to be fully applicable to these subjects, the test would at least give a quantity scale and possibly some indications of differences in writing between left-hand and right-hand subjects, and would provide a sample of the school writing of each of the subjects under similar conditions. In the light of findings on left-handed writing,[2] it was felt that there would be some differences between right- and left-handed subjects in the type of writing they produced, their method of producing it, and also in their speed of writing. In view of the handicaps of the left-handed pupils and the lack of expert guidance on how to overcome them, it seemed probable that such pupils would be incapable of achieving *both* the speed and quality of writing produced by their right-handed contemporaries. Though realising that only a small sample of left-handers would be found in the present investigation, it was felt that valuable guidance for future research on these lines, which would be of practical importance, might be obtained. Further, the study would include most shades of hand-preference, and it was hoped this might make possible some analysis of the relative abilities

---

[1] West, *op cit*   [2] *Supra*, Chapter IX

in writing of the right-hand writers who had a greater or less degree of right-hand dominance. Obviously the best way to standardise the conditions under which the samples were obtained was to set a test such as the following.

DETAILS OF WRITING TEST AND METHOD OF APPLYING

The American Handwriting Scale contains several sample sections of writing, with wording suited to the various ages of children. Each sample is divided into groups of twenty-five letters for ease in checking; and except for the first two samples each passage contains a total of one hundred letters. The sample used in this investigation was that designed for American Sixth Grade children. Copies of the passage were prepared on sheets of paper, one for each child. The passage read as follows:

Teacher gave us writing tests, and found quite a few very poor. Even lazy boys like the drills, and will improve the next time.

This test was administered to the subjects in groups, each class forming a group, and taking approximately one hour to test. The first stage was to make certain that *every* child in the class learnt the section by heart, since, as West pointed out, one cannot make a fair estimate of speed of writing when a child is copying, but only when he is concentrating on the actual writing. Thus, the meaning of the passage was discussed with a class; the words were repeated several times; the first part was then copied three times, or until it was learnt; similarly with the second; then attempts were made to reproduce the whole passage. When it appeared that all the children knew the passage and would not waste time thinking of the correct words, a practice sheet of paper, a pen and ink were issued to each child. Two preliminary attempts were made so that even the dullest children grasped the instructions. It was found that further practice in the passage might be given without boring the subjects. The instructions used were a modified version of those used by West, as they had to be adapted to the language of British children. They were as follows:

I want to see how *quickly* and how *well* you can write. Do not write so quickly that you spoil the writing, nor so slowly that you don't manage to write very much. Just write as you usually do, but do as well as you possibly can. You must only start writing when I say 'Go', and write until I say 'Stop'. If you have written all the story before I say 'Stop', then start and write it all over again. Remember as *quickly* and as *well* as you can.

The time allowed for writing the test was two minutes, which was timed exactly by a stop watch. Twenty seconds before time to start the children were warned to be ready, then care was taken to ascertain that they all started to write exactly on the word 'Go'. Some difficulties were found during the practice attempts. For example, some either started too soon, or too late or stopped when they had completed one attempt, or in some other way did not follow the directions exactly. The final example was written on a separate sheet of paper. Only the test passage was written on one side of the paper, details of the child's name, age, class and school being written on the other side to prevent these from affecting estimates of the writing. When absentees required to be tested after the main groups an attempt was made to keep the conditions comparable with those for the other subjects.

Since all the children in the classes tested for handedness had taken tests for allocation to secondary courses, the schools had in their possession a Promotion Schedule giving the results of the various tests administered. From the schedule were obtained the results of the group intelligence test and achievement tests in English and arithmetic which form part of the battery.

The battery of eighteen tests, the writing test described above, and the information gained from questioning each child on handedness and from the Promotion Schedule, completed the material gathered in the course of the investigation. The following chapters will be devoted to a report of the results of the study and discussion of the findings.

CHAPTER XV

RESULTS OF THE THIRTEEN TESTS
OF
LATERALITY PREFERENCE

TREATMENT OF RESULTS

EACH subject was permitted four trials at each test, a note being made of his preference for right or left at each attempt. Record sheets were prepared detailing the results on all tests for each subject, as 4 (right on all four trials); 3 (right on three trials and left on one); 2 (right on two trials and left on two); 1 (left on three trials and right on one); and 0 (left on all four trials). A total score for hand, foot, ear and eye preference was also obtained for each subject—those for hand, foot and ear ranging from 12 to 0, since there were three tests with four trials in each of these sections, while those for eyedness ranged from 16 to 0, there being four tests in that section. The scores for the individual tests enabled a comparison to be made between both the relative amounts of left and right preference in the different tests, and the correlation between the various tests, or the relative position of the same subject on the different tests. The total scores for each laterality characteristic enabled the same types of comparisons to be made between characteristics as were made between tests.

To allow a comparison of all the tests with one other it was found necessary to divide the scores into two classes, placing all those who showed right preference on all four trials in one class, and all those who had any other score—3, 2, 1 or 0—that is, who showed any tendency other than complete right preference, in the other class. This yielded in each comparison a fourfold table showing those who had complete right preference on the tests being compared, those who were not completely right on both tests, and those for whom the results of the two tests were different. Tables were also drawn up on a threefold

133

classification—R (4), L (0), A (3, 2 or 1)—to facilitate a comparison of the intermediate scores on the tests.

Detailed discussion of the group of left-hand writers will be found in a later chapter. Their results are at this stage included in the total group, as the concern in this chapter is the laterality characteristics of an unselected group. Mention of the results of the left-hand writers is, however, made in passing if they appear to bear on the matter under discussion.

This study of laterality characteristics resulted in some difficulty in finding an admissible statistical method of treating the material, a difficulty which was increased by the choice of a group unselected for hand preference. The inequality of the distribution into the various scores, and in particular the extreme bias towards right in the handedness tests in particular, being in one test 93 per cent of the total, caused obvious difficulties, which even the testing of 330 subjects would not of course overcome. This, when combined with the inability to assume here a continuous variation in laterality characteristics, ruled out many of the better known methods of statistical treatment, since a normal distribution is usually assumed.[1]

The possibility of a sex difference in the frequency of the various laterality characteristics became apparent early, so the

[1] The best method of treating the results seemed, for these reasons, to be by means of calculation of the phi-coefficient since, according to J P Guilford (*Fundamental Statistics in Psychology and Education*, New York: McGraw Hill Book Co Inc, 1950, p 339), this is the most suitable method of comparing two distributions when other methods cannot be applied because of the dichotomous nature of the distributions. He also recommends that the significance of phi when calculated from a fourfold table be determined by a calculation of chi-square, since where it is significant, the corresponding phi is also significant. Unfortunately the maximum size of phi is limited in certain circumstances, circumstances which are present in this study, namely, when the marginal proportions for the two tests are not equal, or nearly so. Thus the maximum phi which could be obtained in many of these tests was well below unity. When studying the underlying strength of the relationship of two tests by means of phi, it is necessary, therefore, to bear in mind the maximal phi possible with these existing marginal totals. As Guilford points out, however, when it is desired to make predictions from these to other categories, then the phi coefficient obtained is a more realistic figure. An approximation of the maximal phi can be ascertained by reading off from the graphic solution given by Guilford (*Ibid*, p 344), which was done in this study, the maximal phi being quoted beside the obtained value in each instance. In the comparisons given in the following part of this chapter, the chi-square values were calculated from fourfold tables, and phi coefficients were got from these by means of the formula ($\phi = \sqrt{\frac{x^2}{N}}$)

percentages of boys and girls who were right, left, and doubtful on each test were calculated, and the significance of the sex differences considered.[1]

The results of the preference tests grouped under the heading of the laterality characteristic they were designed to measure are here presented. The results of each test are detailed, the sex difference discussed, and a comparison made between the results of the various tests of that characteristic. A discussion on the connection between the various tests of one characteristic and those of the others and a series of tables summarising the results of the preference tests are to be found in the following chapter.

DISCUSSION OF THE RESULTS OF THE INDIVIDUAL PREFERENCE TESTS

I HANDEDNESS

A *Screwing*

Most subjects showed a consistent preference for the right hand in this test, the first of the battery to be given (273R and 37L). Only 20 of the subjects (13 boys and 7 girls) changed their preference on subsequent trials, and in several instances this was actually a preference for one hand in unscrewing and the other in screwing. It should be noted that this test may favour right preference by the very nature of the screw, which is more easily unscrewed with the right hand. With a screw, as with many other implements which appear, on the surface, to be symmetrical, there is something in the nature of the design which makes them more adaptable to right hand usage, other examples of this being many kitchen utensils, scissors, and even the fastening on a brooch. The screw on a watch is a more extreme example of this, since its actual position on the watch necessitates the use of the right hand, though it may sometimes be found that a left-hander winds the watch by manipulating it and holding the head of the screw in position, instead of the reverse, a technique which is occasionally employed even when screwing and unscrewing a bottle, as in this test. Though the nature of the screw would probably not affect extreme left-

---

[1] H E Garrett, *Statistics in Psychology and Education*, New York: Longmans, Green and Co Inc, 1947, pp 218-220

handers much, the chances are that those in doubt would prefer the right on later trials. The definite left preference shown on this test represented 11·2 per cent of those tested, yet only 12 of the 18 left-hand writers (5 of 6 girls and 7 of 12 boys) were consistently left in their choice on this test, while 3 were consistently right, the remaining 3 using their right hand on the first three trials, and the left on the last trial.

A greater number of boys than girls showed complete left preference, and also a greater number showed doubtful preference on this test; neither of these differences was, however, great enough to be significant.

B *Reaching*

In this test again nearly all the subjects showed a consistent preference, in most instances for the right hand. Out of 330 subjects, 274 used the right hand and 27 used the left hand on all trials of this test.

The most noticeable difference between this test and the previous one was the larger number who were, here, equally divided between left and right, 16 here against 5 in the Screwing Test. Since no skill or strength was required in the Reaching Test, nor was there anything particularly leading to right preference, as there was in the previous test, those who were doubtful found nothing in the test to encourage them to come down on one side or the other. Only half of the left-hand writers used the left hand consistently in this test.

The same tendency for the boys to show more left preference than the girls was again evident in this test, while the percentages of those who were doubtful on the test were almost identical for the two. The difference between the percentage of boys and girls showing consistent left preference was large enough to be significant at the ·05 level of significance.

C *Throwing*

Few subjects were in any doubt as to their preferred hand for throwing, 3 only out of 330 showed any inconsistency in their scores on the four trials; of the others, 307 preferred the right and 20 the left hand. A practised activity such as this, and one requiring a certain amount of skill and accuracy, seemed to divide the subjects almost entirely into two groups, their throwing hand having been determined years before. Since accuracy and the competitive element were stressed in the test, this would obviously not lead the subjects to indulge in any experimentation with the hand used. Left preference was shown by 6·1 per cent of the total group of subjects, and by all but three of the left-hand writers.

Left preference was again higher among the boys, but the difference was, however, not great enough to be significant.

D Correlation between the Tests of Handedness

The values of chi-square and of phi were obtained when a comparison was made between those showing complete right preference, and those showing any left preference on the three tests. All the chi-square results were significant well beyond the one per cent level, revealing a high probability of a connection between the tests. The values of phi obtained, though limited by the nature of the distribution of the scores, were high enough to be significant. The Screwing and Throwing Tests had the highest measure of agreement, as can be inferred from Table III.

TABLE III

CORRELATION BETWEEN TESTS OF HAND PREFERENCE
(330 SUBJECTS)

Tests	χ^2	P	ϕ	Maximum ϕ
Screwing Reaching	19·4	<·01	·24	·98
Reaching Throwing	33·9	<·01	·32	·57
Throwing Screwing	63·8	<·01	·44	·57

II FOOTEDNESS

A Kicking

The results of this test clearly reveal that most subjects were in no doubt regarding their preferred foot for kicking, 7 only showing any inconsistency, and that for most of the subjects the preferred foot was the right (301R, 22L). This activity, like throwing, is a much practised one, particularly by the boys, and for that reason one in which they would have established their preference long before the testing. The emphasis on skill in this test would prevent the subjects experimenting with the non-preferred foot, since, so far as they were aware, the aim of the test was to ascertain how many times they could kick the ball between the legs of a chair. None of the subjects used the right and left foot an equal number of times.

Consistent left preference was slightly greater among the boys than the girls, as also was any degree of left preference. Neither difference was, however, great enough to be statistically significant.

B *Stepping*

The pattern of results on this test was completely different from that found in the previous tests. The results here were much more evenly divided into the five categories, 104 subjects showing inconsistency, or almost half as many as were consistent on all four trials. The amount of consistent left preference was also considerably higher on this test (165R, 61L).

The boys again showed a greater incidence of consistent left preference on this test than did the girls, and also of those showing any degree of left preference. These differences were both great enough to be significant.

Only 6 of 18 left-hand writers were consistently left on this test. This, when combined with the unusual distribution found in the total group, which was so different from that on any of the other tests, led to suspicions about the test, suspicions which were later confirmed when the test was compared with the other tests. Though the actual situation in this test was one which few of the subjects would have encountered previously, the training which they received in stepping off with a certain foot had, it seemed, caused a distortion of the distribution. The insistence in many situations that boys step with the left foot in marching and dancing, for example, had, it was felt, also widened the gap between the two sexes, and went far to explain its greater significance in this test than in the other tests.

C *Hopping*

The results of this test revealed that in Hopping the majority of subjects, both boys and girls, had a consistent preference for the right foot (247R, 57L). The number showing consistent left-preference in this test was comparable to that in the Stepping Test, but there was less inconsistency in choice of foot here than in that test.

Both partial and complete preference was less with the boys than with the girls in the Hopping test, which was the reverse of the finding on the other tests. The sex difference in left preference was not, however, great enough to be significant; while the difference between boys and girls showing inconsistency was barely significant ($P = \cdot05$).

D *Correlation between the Tests of Footedness*

There appeared to be no correlation between the Tests of Kicking and Stepping, and between those of Stepping and Hopping whereas comparison between the tests of Kicking and Hopping indicated the probability of a significant correlation between the two tests.

TABLE IV

CORRELATION BETWEEN TESTS OF FOOT PREFERENCE
(330 SUBJECTS)

Tests	χ^2	P	ϕ	Maximum ϕ
Kicking Stepping	$\cdot94$	$\cdot50$	$\cdot05$	$\cdot31$
Stepping Hopping	$\cdot14$	$\cdot80$	$\cdot02$	$\cdot58$
Kicking Hopping	$15\cdot2$	$<\cdot01$	$\cdot22$	$\cdot53$

Stepping appears to be the test in this group which disagrees with the results of the other tests. It was felt that this might arise from the large number who were undecided on that test and who, in drawing up the fourfold tables, were placed in the category with left preference. For that reason a further analysis was made of the results of this test. Taking the Hopping and Stepping Tests and comparing them, since the numbers showing consistent left preference on these two tests were comparable

(57 and 61 subjects respectively), it was found that 28 subjects were consistently right in stepping and consistently left in hopping; while 46 were consistently left in stepping and consistently right in hopping.

III EAREDNESS

A *Sound in Box*

On the results of this test about one-third of the subjects showed consistent left preference, most of the remainder being consistently right (198R, 114L). Though this was an unpractised activity, few changed their preference from one trial to the next, only 9 boys and 9 girls being undecided. It seems, therefore, that there must be a preferred ear even in a situation such as this where external circumstances favoured neither. The subject placed his ear down to the box to listen for the watch, without touching it, thus ruling out the possibility that the preferred hand might influence the results. In spite of these precautions, the tendency on this test, as on tests of handedness, was for the majority to show right preference. Here, however, the balance in favour of right preference was not so extreme, being roughly 3:2 instead of 5:1 as in the Reaching Test which was probably the most comparable test of hand preference. The extent to which the results were determined or affected by the relative aural acuity of the two ears has not been established in this present study.

Left preference was again shown by a greater number of the boys than girls as in the tests of handedness, but the difference was not significant.

B *Stop Watch*

The majority of the subjects (271) showed right preference on this test of earedness, the remainder being fairly evenly divided between mixed preference and consistent left preference (25 and 34 respectively). Most of those who were not consistently right or left used the right and left ear an equal number of times. In this test the subjects held the watch to whichever ear they preferred, with whichever hand they pleased, in order that the effect of the dominant hand on the results might be ascertained. As may be seen from a comparison of this test and the previous test where handedness did not enter, the number showing consistent left preference was reduced by more than two-thirds (from 34·5 per cent to 10·3 per cent). In most instances the watch was held to the ear with the corresponding hand, even when that was not the preferred hand in any of the preference tests of handedness. Even those who used the left ear twice and the right ear for the other two trials, still used the corresponding hand in each trial. Rarely was crossed preference shown. The emphasis on speed on this test may have reduced slightly the number showing crossed preference of hand and ear from the number who would use a different hand and ear in a real life situation, such as telephoning. Probably in using the telephone the situation is still further complicated for some people who may find it necessary to write with the hand that is already occupied in holding the receiver. Rarely under such circumstances does a person change the receiver to the other ear to suit the hand now being used. Thus, the crossed position there is probably the result of a series of circumstances and not the initial one.

A sex difference was also evident on this test, in favour of greater left preference on the part of the boys, the difference between the percentage of boys and the percentage of girls showing consistent left preference on this test being significant at the 5 per cent level.

C *Head Turning*

From the results of this test it appears that most of the subjects had a consistent preference for one side or the other when turning their heads in response to a sound made immediately behind them, and that for the majority, the preference was for the right, 230 subjects preferring the right and 88 subjects showing consistent left preference. The amount of consistent left preference shown on this test, though greater than that shown in the Stop Watch Test (34L) was not as great as that shown in the Sound in Box Test (114L). Fewer were inconsistent on this test than on either of the other tests of earedness.

The sex difference in this test was again in favour of greater left preference on the part of the boys, though the difference was not significant.

D *Correlation between the Tests of Earedness*

From the values of chi-square and phi a comparison was made between the three tests of earedness. The probability of a significant correlation between the Sound in Box Test and the Stop Watch Tests was shown. The value of chi-square obtained on the Sound in Box and Head Turning Tests also indicated the probability of a significant correlation between these tests. The third comparison, that between the Stop Watch and Head Turning Tests, failed to establish a significant correlation between the tests.

TABLE V

CORRELATION BETWEEN TESTS OF EAR PREFERENCE
(330 SUBJECTS)

Tests	χ^2	P	ϕ	Maximum ϕ
Sound in Box Stop Watch	26·0	<·01	·28	·58
Sound in Box Head Turning	5·98	·02	·14	·81
Stop Watch Head Turning	1·64	·30	·07	·71

There appears, from these results, to be a definite correlation between the preference of the subjects on the two selected tests of earedness, Sound in Box and Stop Watch Tests. The Head Turning Test which involved turning round after a sound had been made, was not an instinctive reaction to the sound, but rather a deliberate act following it. This test appeared to have little correlation with the preferences found on the other tests of earedness. There was a slight correlation between it and the Sound in Box Test, but none with the Stop Watch Test where handedness was also involved.

IV EYEDNESS

A *Cone Test*

The numbers of subjects showing consistent right and left preference on this test were 184 and 110 respectively. Those showing inconsistency were fairly evenly divided into the three categories of scores 3, 2 and 1, the frequencies being 16, 10 and

10 respectively. The distribution of the scores of boys and girls was practically the same on this test. Thus most subjects had a consistent preference for one eye or the other on this test (only 36 were not consistent), and for the majority the preference was for the right eye.

B *Hole in Card*

In this test, as in the previous one, the subjects were unaware that a choice of eye was involved, as both eyes remained open. The distribution of scores on this test was similar to that on the Cone Test, except that slightly fewer subjects were inconsistent on this one, resulting in a slight increase both in those with consistent right and with consistent left preference, the numbers here being 199 and 120 respectively. There was no significant sex difference on this test.

C *Peep Show*

The subjects were clearly divided into two classes on this test, those showing consistent right preference and those showing consistent left preference, 208 and 122 respectively. The percentages of boys and girls showing consistent left preference on this test were practically identical.

The subjects were unaware that the eye selected in this test was being noted, and were under the impression that the task was to read the words written inside the box. Yet they were consistent in their eye preference on all four trials.

D *Cylinder Test*

This test, like the previous one, involved a deliberate choice of one eye, and here again most subjects showed a consistent preference, only 6 subjects giving different results on successive trials. Consistent right preference was shown by 205 and consistent left preference by 119 of the subjects, figures very similar to those obtained on the Peep Show Test. The scores obtained by boys and girls in this test were very similar.

E *Correlation between the Tests of Eyedness*

All the values of chi-square obtained when a comparison was made between the tests of eyedness were significant well beyond

L

the one per cent level; the corresponding values of phi are accordingly significant.

TABLE VI

CORRELATION BETWEEN TESTS OF EYE PREFERENCE
(330 SUBJECTS)

Tests	χ^2	P	ϕ	Maximum ϕ
Cone Peep Show	160·4	<·01	·70	·86
Cone Cylinder	144·9	<·01	·66	·87
Hole in Card Cylinder	209·5	<·01	·80	·96
Cone Hole in Card	191·0	<·01	·76	·91
Hole in Card Peep Show	233·1	<·01	·84	·93
Peep Show Cylinder	261·7	<·01	·89	·97

The more even distribution between left and right preference obtained in tests of eyedness resulted in higher maximum values of phi, and is one explanation of the higher correlations obtained on these tests than on any involving handedness. The correlations between all four tests of eyedness were very high, especially in view of the precautions which were taken to prevent any test influencing the subsequent tests. When one considers the high correlations obtained here between the tests of eyedness, and also the internal consistency of the tests, it seems impossible to deny that these appear to indicate the existence of eyedness as a laterality characteristic. Study of the results of all four tests of eyedness revealed that 246 subjects had consistent results on all four trials of all four tests, 160 being consistently right and 86 showing consistently left preference.

The percentage of boys showing consistent left preference on all four tests of eyedness was 25·9 and the percentage of girls 26·2 per cent; while 50·0 per cent of the boys and 53·0 per cent of the girls showed some left tendency. These differences between the results for boys and girls on the tests of eyedness were not great enough to be significant.

CHAPTER XVI

COMPARISON OF LATERALITY CHARACTERISTICS AS MEASURED BY PREFERENCE TESTS

THE comparison of the tests of the various laterality characteristics, both the relative percentages of the various preferences found and the correlations between the tests, will now be considered.

The percentage frequency of each type of preference in all thirteen tests is given in Table VII.

TABLE VII

PERCENTAGES OF SUBJECTS SHOWING VARIOUS PREFERENCES ON THE PREFERENCE TESTS (330 SUBJECTS)

Tests		Percentage of Subjects[1]		
Type of Test	*Name of Test*	*R*	*A*	*L*
Hand	Screwing	82·7	6·1	11·2
	Reaching	83·0	8·8	8·2
	Throwing	93·0	·9	6·1
Foot	Kicking	91·2	2·1	6·7
	Stepping	50·3	31·5	18·2
	Hopping	74·8	7·9	17·3
Ear	Sound in Box	60·0	5·5	34·5
	Stop Watch	82·1	7·6	10·3
	Head Turning	69·7	3·6	26·7
Eye	Cone	55·8	10·9	33·3
	Hole in Card	60·3	3·3	36·4
	Peep Show	63·0	0	37·0
	Cylinder	62·1	1·8	36·1

[1] *R*—Right on all 4 trials; *L*—Left on all 4 trials; *A*—all other scores

HANDEDNESS AND FOOTEDNESS

Since the inter-correlations on the tests of footedness were not very high, it was decided to compare the tests individually with those of handedness instead of treating them collectively as a single score. As was shown in the previous chapter, the Stepping Test did not appear to be a reliable test of footedness, and for that reason it is not considered further in this section. The results obtained from calculation of chi-square and phi on the other tests are presented in Table VIII.

TABLE VIII

CORRELATION BETWEEN KICKING AND HOPPING TESTS AND HANDEDNESS TESTS (330 SUBJECTS)

Tests	χ^2	P	ϕ	Maximum ϕ
Kicking Screwing	51·9	<·01	·40	·68
Kicking Reaching	17·7	<·01	·23	·68
Kicking Throwing	71·2	<·01	·46	·85
Hopping Screwing	6·7	<·01	·14	·78
Hopping Reaching	0·46	<·50	·04	·78
Hopping Throwing	12·9	<·01	·20	·46

When the Kicking Test of footedness was compared with each test of handedness the value of chi-square was in each instance significant well beyond the ·01 per cent level. Thus all three values of phi were significant. The correlation between the Kicking and Throwing Tests (ϕ ·46 max ϕ ·85) compared favourably with the intercorrelations found on the handedness tests.

The values of chi-square obtained when the Hopping Test was compared with the handedness tests were significant beyond the one per cent level in two instances, with the Screwing and Throwing Tests. The value of chi-square found on the Reaching and Hopping showed that there was practically no relationship between them. Since the values of chi-square between the Hopping Test and the Throwing and Screwing Tests were significant the corresponding value of phi were also significant.

These were, however, lower than those found when the Kicking Test was compared with the corresponding tests of handedness.

HANDEDNESS AND EAREDNESS

A comparison between the percentage of left and right preference found on the handedness tests and those on the various earedness tests (see Table VII) showed, as would be expected, that the percentages in the Stop Watch Test of earedness are closest to those of handedness. This test had also the highest correlation with the handedness tests as may be seen in Table IX.

TABLE IX

CORRELATION BETWEEN TESTS OF HAND AND EAR
PREFERENCE (330 SUBJECTS)

Tests	χ^2	P	ϕ	Maximum ϕ
Handedness Sound in Box	1·9	·20	·08	·78
Handedness Stop Watch	15·1	<·01	·21	·73
Handedness Head Turning	6·4	·02	·14	·95

The values of chi-square found on a comparison of the results of the handedness tests with the Stop Watch Test and the Head Turning Tests were significant and thus the corresponding values of phi were also significant. The chi-square obtained on comparing the handedness tests with the Sound in Box Test of earedness indicated that there was no significant relationship between them.

The results of this study suggested some connection between the ear selected for listening when an object is held in the hand, and the hand used in preference tests of handedness, and a low but significant correlation between the dominant hand and the direction in which the head is turned on hearing a sound. No significant connection was found between the ear preferred and the hand used in preference tests of handedness when the subject was not permitted to touch the watch.

HANDEDNESS AND EYEDNESS

In all three tests of handedness and in all four tests of eyedness the majority of subjects showed right preference. The proportion of right to left preference was different in the two groups of tests. In the hand preference tests it was approximately 5:1; while in the eye preference tests it was approximately 3:2. Details of the relation between the results of subjects on the two groups of tests may be seen in Table X.

TABLE X

RELATION BETWEEN THE RESULTS ON TESTS OF HAND AND EYE PREFERENCE

(*Figures in the body of the table are numbers of pupils*)

Eye Tests	Hand Tests			
	Right (*Score* 12)	Doubtful (*Score* 11-1)	Left (*Score* 0)	Totals
Right (Score 16)	121	39	0	160
Doubtful (Score 15-1)	55	24	5	84
Left (Score 0)	60	23	3	86
Totals	236	86	8	330

The values of chi-square and phi calculated for these groups of tests from a fourfold table are given below in Table XI.

TABLE XI

CORRELATION BETWEEN TESTS OF HAND AND EYE PREFERENCE (330 SUBJECTS)

Tests	χ^2	P	ϕ	Maximum ϕ
Handedness Eyedness (Consistently Right, Not Right)	2·6	·20	·09	·65
Handedness Eyedness (Consistent, Not Consistent)	0·33	·70	·03	·98

The value of chi-square obtained between those consistently right and those not right on the tests of handedness and eyedness was not significant.

The second comparison in the table is between those who were consistent and those who were not consistent on the two groups of tests to ascertain whether there was a tendency for those who were doubtful on handedness tests also to be doubtful on eyedness tests. The chi-square value for this comparison indicates the absence of any such tendency.

There were 122 of the total 330 subjects who were dominantly right or left on all trials of all tests of either hand or eye and doubtful on the other group of tests; while lack of consistency on both groups of tests was shown by 24 subjects. No subjects who were left on all tests of hand preference were right-eyed on all eyedness tests.

No connection between eyedness and handedness was found on the tests employed in this study; nor did inconsistency in one group of tests seem to be connected with the inconsistency in the other.

An analysis of the Intelligence Quotients of the 24 subjects (8 girls and 16 boys) who gave inconsistent results on the tests of both eyedness and handedness revealed no sign that they were of less than average intelligence. The mean I Q of these subjects was 109·3 which was almost identical with that of the total group of right-handed subjects (109·3 for girls, 109·4 for boys) and further, only two of them had an I Q of under 100.

EYEDNESS AND EAREDNESS

The percentage of left and right dominance for eyedness and the Sound in Box Test of earedness were comparable, as may be seen from Table XII.

TABLE XII

CORRELATION BETWEEN TESTS OF EAR AND EYE
PREFERENCE (330 SUBJECTS)

Tests	χ^2	P	ϕ	Maximum ϕ
Eyedness Sound in Box	7·3	<·01	·15	·85
Eyedness Stop Watch	2·6	·20	·09	·50
Eyedness Head Turning	0·36	·70	·03	·67

The value of chi-square obtained between the eyedness and the Sound in Box Test implies that the corresponding value of phi is also significant, indicating a low, but positive correlation between eyedness and the Sound in Box Test. The values of chi-square found between eyedness and the Stop Watch Test and eyedness and the Head Turning Test do not justify us in assuming any relationship between the tests.

The relative percentages of right, left and doubtful preference on all the preference tests are shown in Table VII, while the correlations discussed in this and the preceding chapter are summarised in Table XIII. The correlations have been assumed to be significant where the corresponding value of chi-square was significant.

TABLE XIII

CORRELATION BETWEEN PREFERENCE TESTS (330 SUBJECTS)[1]

		Hand			Foot			Ear			Eye			
		Sc	Re	Th	Ki	St	Ho	SB	SW	HT	Co	HC	PS	Cy
Hand	Sc		34	44	40		14							
	Re	98		32	23		04	08	21	14		09		
	Th	57	57		46		10							
Foot	Ki	68	68	85		05	22							
	St				31		02							
	Ho	78	78	46	53	58								
Ear	SB		78						28	14		15		
	SW		73					58		07		09		
	HT		95					81	71			03		
Eye	Co											76	70	66
	HC		65					85	50	67	91		34	83
	PS										86	93		59
	Cy										87	96	97	

[1] Figures above diagonal are phi coefficients obtained; (corresponding figures below diagonal are maximum phi coefficients). Shaded sections indicate significant correlations

[2] Key to Test Names:
Hand: Sc—Screwing, Re—Reaching, Th—Throwing
Foot: Ki—Kicking, St—Stepping, Ho—Hopping
Ear: SB—Sound in Box, SW—Stop Watch, HT—Head Turning
Eye: Co—Cone, HC—Hole in Card, PS—Peep Show, Cy—Cylinder.

CHAPTER XVII

RESULTS OF THE SPEED OF CROSSING TEST

METHOD OF TREATING RESULTS

DETAILS of the method of applying the Speed of Crossing Test, the ninth test to be administered, were set out in Chapter XIV. The scores obtained took the form of the number of crosses drawn by each subject with right hand and left at the first and second trials. In order to make the results comparable for all subjects with regard to writing and non-writing hand, the writing hand was tested first in each instance, 18 out of 330 subjects (12 boys and 6 girls) making their first attempt with the left hand and their second attempt with the right. For each subject the total score for the right and left hand was calculated. This enabled a comparison to be made between the absolute ability of different subjects with their writing hand, and particularly between the left- and right-hand writers. An Index of Handedness was then calculated for each subject based on the ratio of his score with right hand to his score with his left hand —thus right-handedness was represented by an index above unity, left-handedness by an index below unity, and ambidexterity by unity. A comparison could therefore be made of the relative ability of the two hands for different subjects.

COMPARISON OF SCORES OF RIGHT- AND LEFT-HANDERS

The average scores with right and left hand for the total group of subjects are as follows:

Boys (162) Right Hand 53·7; Left Hand 37·5
Girls (168) Right Hand 60·2; Left Hand 39·3

From this it is apparent that the average scores obtained by the girls, both with right and left hand, were higher than those of the boys. To make the analysis of the difference fairer the scores of the left-hand writers were excluded, since there were

12 boys and only 6 girls in this group, and these were considered separately.

TABLE XIV

FREQUENCY DISTRIBUTION OF SCORES WITH WRITING HAND ON SPEED
OF CROSSING TEST

| | Frequencies | | | | |
| | Right-Hand Writers | | Left-Hand Writers | | |
Scores	Boys	Girls	Boys	Girls	Total
75–79	–	3	–	–	3
70–74	3	17	–	–	20
65–69	12	38	–	1	51
60–64	26	40	1	3	70
55–59	46	32	2	2	82
50–54	28	17	5	–	50
45–49	19	11	2	–	32
40–44	11	4	2	–	17
35–39	5	–	–	–	5
Total	150	162	12	6	330

Table XIV shows the frequency distribution of the right-hand writers on this test when using their writing hand, and also the corresponding scores of the left-handers with their writing hand, the left. The standard deviation from the mean was the same for both the right-handed boys and girls (S D, 7·75). A significant sex difference between the means of right-handed boys and girls was found on this test (Diff, 6·0, S E of Diff, 0·88). In view of this difference it seemed advisable to compare the scores obtained by the left-hand writers with those obtained by right-hand writers *of the same sex* with their writing hand. Such a comparison showed that, of the left-handed girls, 4 obtained scores below, and 2 above the mean for right-handed girls (Mean 61·5); while among the left-handed boys, 10 had scores below and 2 above the mean for right-handed boys (Mean 55·5). Though the left-handed group here was, admittedly, small, it can at least be said that there was a tendency for the left-handers to make a poorer score with their left hand than did right-handers with their right.

INDEX OF HANDEDNESS

TABLE XV

FREQUENCY DISTRIBUTION OF RATIO OF WRITING HAND TO NON-
WRITING HAND ON SPEED OF CROSSING TEST

| | Frequencies | | | | |
| | Right-Hand Writers | | Left-Hand Writers | | |
Index	Boys	Girls	Boys	Girls	Total
2·5–2·59	1	1			2
2·4–2·49	–	–			0
2·3–2·39	–	–			0
2·2–2·29	–	1			1
2·1–2·19	–	1			1
2·0–2·09	6	7			13
1·9–1·99	4	8			12
1·8–1·89	6	12			18
1·7–1·79	8	19	–	–	27
1·6–1·69	17	22		1	40
1·5–1·59	37	32		–	69
1·4–1·49	35	31	2	1	69
1·3–1·39	19	18	3	3	43
1·2–1·29	5	8	5	1	19
1·1–1·19	11	2	1	–	14
1·0–1·09	–	–	1	–	1
0·9–0·99	1	–			1
Total	150	162	12	6	330

Details of the range of indices found among the right-hand
writers given above show that there was a slight tendency for
the girls to score a higher index than the boys—indicating a
greater ability with the right hand relative to the left. The mean
index for the right-handed girls was 1·6 (S D ·23), and for the
right-handed boys it was 1·52 (S D ·23). The difference between these means was great enough to be significant well
beyond the one per cent level of significance (C R 3·07). In
order to compare the magnitude of these indices and those of
the left-hand writers, it was decided in this latter instance, also,

to calculate an index of ratio of writing hand to non-writing hand. A comparison of the relative ability of the writing hand to the other with regard to right- and left-handers was felt to be necessary in view of the suggestion made by many that in left-handers the superiority of the left hand over the right is not as great as the superiority of right over left in right-handers. It may be seen from Table XV, where these indices are set out, that the ratios tended to be smaller in the left-handed group. It was found that not one of the group of left-hand writers had a ratio of writing hand to non-writing hand larger than the mean for right-handers of the same sex.

It would appear, therefore, that there is some truth in the view that the degree of dominance with regard to speed, or the distance from ambidexterity, is on the average greater in right-handed persons than in left-handers. Though superficially this may seem surprising, a little consideration suggests the explanation. In a right-handed world there are occasions on which even the extreme left-hander finds it necessary to employ the right hand, while the reverse is seldom true for right-handers. Further, practically without exception, left-handers are at some time forced into actually attempting to write with the right hand for a period, which thus results in a narrower margin between the performance of the two hands in comparison with that of right-handers.

In view of the lack of incentive to right-handers to utilise the left hand for writing at any time, it is surprising to find so many right-handers with a low index of handedness, or who are, in other words, almost as good or as bad with both hands. Table XV reveals that 12 right-handed boys and 2 right-handed girls had an index of less than 1·2, one boy actually scoring better with his left hand. It should be borne in mind that a low index does not necessarily mean a low score, indicating only comparable scores with both hands, which may be low, high or intermediate. If a right-handed person is extremely good with both hands he is, however, less likely to attempt to use his left hand than is someone who is poor with the right. On consideration of these 14 subjects scoring an index of less than 1·2, it was found that only two, one boy and one girl, were left-handed, the girl in everything but writing and the boy even at times in writing, while the remainder had never, so far as they could remember, written with the left hand. When the score obtained with the right hand by these 14 subjects was considered it was found that all but three (two being those mentioned above) had a score below the mean for the group of their own sex. Thus the low index was not to be explained by two exceptionally good hands. It must either be assumed that the transfer had, for them, been considerable from right to left hand, or that little profit had accrued to the right hand from all the practice it had received. Possibly the increase in left-hand writers appearing as the attitude to left-handedness becomes more tolerant, involves children in a comparable position to the group discussed here, who would then use the left hand for writing, especially if this narrow margin between the two hands is combined with a preference for the left.

COMPARISON OF SPEED OF CROSSING AND HAND PREFERENCE TESTS

A comparison of the Index of Handedness on the Speed of Crossing Test and the degree of preference on the tests of Hand Preference (Screwing, Reaching and Throwing), was difficult because the distribution of subjects was so different in the two aspects, relative ability and preference. The great majority of right-hand writers showed right preference on all three tests, and only a few on two tests or one—the figures being 235, 61 and 16 showing right preference on all trials of all three tests, on two tests, and on one or no test, respectively. On the Speed of Crossing Test the indices of the right-hand writers were more normally distributed.

A study of all those who *did not* score complete right-handedness on the preference tests (77 subjects) revealed that they tended to have lower indices of handedness than those who were right handers on all the preference tests (235 subjects). In the group showing some left preference there were twice as many with an index near to left-handedness as there were at the other extreme; by contrast, in the group showing no left preference there were almost twice as many with a high index as there were with a low index. A direct comparison was difficult because of the disparity in numbers, but a study of the percentages of subjects at the extremes with regard to index (below 1·4 and above 1·7), as shown in Table XVI, reveals their relative position on the preference tests.

TABLE XVI

COMPARISON OF PREFERENCE TEST RESULTS OF SUBJECTS WITH HIGH OR LOW INDICES ON SPEED OF CROSSING TEST (AS PERCENTAGES)

Speed of Crossing	Preference Right on all Tests	Test Result Not Right on all Tests
Index Below 1·4	15·3 per cent	36·4 per cent
Index Above 1·7	26·0 per cent	16·9 per cent
Total Number of Subjects	235	77

The difference in the percentages in the two preference groups with regard to their index, shows that there was a difference of 21·1 per cent between those with a low index. This difference was great enough to be significant (S E of Diff, 6·0). The percentage of those with a high degree of preference who had a high index was larger than that of those who showed any left preference. Here, however, the difference was not so large (9·1 per cent, C R, 1·77).

One explanation of the absence of a more exact connection between these two aspects, and of the existence of as many as 36 subjects with an index of less than 1·4 who still used their right hand on all preference tests, is the fact already mentioned that some of these, having a high ability with both hands, have in a right-handed world no particular urge to utilise the latent ability of the left hand. An analysis of those who, though right-hand writers, showed a preference for the left on two or more of the tests and an Index of Handedness of less than 1·4 (10 subjects, 5 boys and 5 girls) shows that four of them, three girls and one boy, had actually been left-hand writers at some time and had changed or been changed to the right hand, retaining their preference for the left in other activities and showing a narrow margin between scores with the left and right hand in a speed test.

This test gives a clearer picture of the relative speed of right- and left-handers than can be obtained from a writing test in the usual sense of the word, where the relative emphasis placed by the child on quality acts as a complicating factor. A comparison between the scores obtained on this test of Speed of Crossing and on speed in the Writing Test will be presented in Chapter XIX.

CHAPTER XVIII

RESULTS OF THE SIMULTANEOUS WRITING AND VAN RIPER TESTS

THE Simultaneous Writing Test and the testing by the Van Riper Critical Angle Board, both involving bimanual drawing, have sufficient in common to justify their consideration in the same chapter. The Simultaneous Writing Test involved writing a series of numerals with both hands at the same time and with visual cues removed, thus enabling a study to be made of the instances in which mirroring of the numerals resulted and with which hand this was performed. This test was a simplified and somewhat cruder approach to the problem than that provided by the Van Riper apparatus, where a further distraction was introduced, one whose influence was gradually increased. The writing was, on this latter test, done in a vertical position by copying a diagram, but still without visual cues as to direction, since the subject, though he had not his eyes shut in this test, was not permitted to look at the paper on which he was drawing. The difficulty was increased as the vertical boards were rotated back 30 degrees between each attempt. Thus it was not only possible here to determine whether mirroring took place, and if so, with which hand and with which diagram there was a greater amount, but also to consider the point at which the mirroring took place by the angle of the verticle boards.

The results of the two tests will be discussed separately, then compared, and finally evaluated in the light of the other information gained in the course of the study.

SIMULTANEOUS WRITING TEST

Two attempts were made at this test by each subject, the seven numerals being written at each attempt. Only asymmetrical figures were included, hence the exclusion of 0, 1 and 8. The remaining seven were repeated quickly to the subject who, with eyes closed, wrote them down with both hands at the same time. It was possible to note at the time whether any numeral was mirrored and also to go back and check the results at a later date. The order in which the numbers were written down was that normal to the subject, viz: 2, 3, 4, 5, 6, 7, 9. Speed was emphasised in order to prevent awareness of an error from resulting in its correction. Any suggestion of mirroring was counted, even when corrected, since that was taken to indicate its presence.

The anticipated result for a right-handed subject was mirroring with the *left* hand, while a left-handed subject was expected to mirror with the *right* hand. In spite of the existence of only 18 left-handed writers in the group there was a considerable amount of mirroring with the right hand—approximately one-sixth of that with the left hand.

TABLE XVII

NUMBER OF SUBJECTS PRODUCING MIRROR-IMAGE IN SIMULTANEOUS
WRITING TEST

Number of Subjects Mirroring

	Left Hand Only	Right Hand Only	Both	Neither	Total
Right-Hand Writers					
Boys	83	4	17	46	150
Girls	77	4	26	55	162
Total	160	8	43	101	312
Left-Hand Writers					
Boys	–	5	2	5	12
Girls	–	4	–	2	6
Total	–	9	2	7	18

Details are presented in Table XVII of the actual numbers of subjects mirroring with the left hand, right hand, both hands either together or at different points in the test, and the total who mirrored with neither. One-third of the subjects contributed no mirroring to the results, while 45 subjects mirrored with both hands.

It will be seen from the table that nine of the left-handed

M

subjects first mirrored with the right hand only, and seven with neither, both results which might have been expected. However, the remaining two mirrored with both hands. On studying their results it was found that one had mirrored once with each hand, the same number at the same time; while the other mirrored with the left twice in the first trial and once in the second, and once with the right in the second, not at the same time. This latter subject's result was of interest in view of his score on the Speed of Crossing Test where he had an Index of Handedness of unity, indicating equal skill with both hands.

A study of the eight right-handed subjects who mirrored with the right hand revealed that only one of them mirrored more than one numeral, while one of the girls was actually left-handed in all but writing. The record sheets of the 17 boys who mirrored with both hands revealed that ten mirrored only once with the right hand and the rest of the time with the left, and four mirrored only twice with the right, which is only an average of once per trial. A consideration of the remaining three whose mirroring in the right and left was 4, 12; 5, 6; and 4, 1 respectively, showed that the first (score 4, 12) was actually a changed left-hander, having been forced to use his right hand in school. The boy scoring 5, 6 actually mirrored with both hands at the same time (with one additional mirroring with the left only); while the third (4, 1) was actually left-handed in his preference on the Screwing Test. An analysis of the results of the 26 girls who mirrored with both showed that 17 mirrored twice or less with the right hand. Of the remaining nine, two had been left-hand writers, and another was left-handed in screwing. It seemed advisable to make a comparison between these results and those of the Van Riper Test before any final conclusions were drawn.

It is clear that even in children of the age here tested, eleven plus, when the visual cues were removed there was a tendency to mirror with the non-writing hand. Among the right-hand writers (312) there were 51 who mirrored with either the right hand or both hands at some time during the test, including five subjects who had strong left tendencies, all but one having written with the left hand at some time. It should be noted that not one of the left-hand writers produced a mirror-image with the left hand only, and only two with the left hand at all, indicating that even with the visual cues removed they had still sufficient control over the direction of movement of the left hand to prevent it from mirroring. Possibly some mirroring with the left hand might have been found in younger left-handed subjects with, as in this test, the removal of visual cues to direction.

THE VAN RIPER TEST

I GENERAL DISCUSSION

Four diagrams were used in this test,[1] the first being a very simple visual pattern; the second, the number 'three' presented as an auditory stimulus; while the third and fourth patterns were a more complicated design presented in two different positions. The results noted were, for each diagram, and at each angle, whether there was any mirroring, and if so, whether by the right or left hand.

The results indicated that, with each diagram, as the angle boards were rotated back from zero to 180 degrees the amount of mirroring increased. Further, it was found that the total mirroring with the two hands (R + L) of both boys and girls increased with each diagram; while the proportion of right to left mirroring was greatest for Diagram 2, the auditory diagram, which, because of the method of presentation, had to be a pattern with which the writing-hand was already familiar.

In Van Riper's original method of using the apparatus he continued only until an angle was reached where mirroring took place plus one stage further to make certain of its consistency. The first angle at which the mirroring took place was then taken as the 'Critical Angle', and the hand mirroring as the non-dominant hand. In this present study, following the example of Smith,[2] each subject was tested through four angles in order to ascertain the consistency of the first results. The results stated in Table XVIII were calculated on the basis of the total mirroring at all angles and on all four diagrams.

[1] See Figure 7, page 125, for illustration of the diagrams
[2] L C Smith, 'A Study of Laterality Characteristics of Retarded Readers and Reading Achievers'

TABLE XVIII

DOMINANT HANDEDNESS AS MEASURED BY TOTAL MIRRORING ON THE
VAN RIPER TEST (ALL SUBJECTS)

Number of Subjects[1]

	Right Dominance	Left Dominance	Ambi	Total
Right-Hand Writers				
Boys	95	37	18	150
Girls	113	40	9	162
Total	208	77	27	312
Left-Hand Writers				
Boys	3	9	0	12
Girls	3	3	0	6
Total	6	12	0	18

From the table it may be seen that even on that rough criterion
not all left-hand writers, who may be assumed to be the more
extreme left-handers, were differentiated, only two-thirds of
them mirroring with the right hand more than the left. A more
rigid criterion was set up and dominance then determined by
the hand mirroring consistently on all diagrams, and at all
angles at which mirroring actually took place. The results are
set forth in Table XIX where details are also given of the subjects who were consistent on all four diagrams on Van Riper's
criterion, namely, those who mirrored first with the same hand
on each diagram. It may be seen that 116 of the right-handed
subjects produced the results expected, namely, left-hand
mirroring, or in 4 instances no mirroring with either hand;
while 7 left-handers gained the expected result of right-hand
mirroring. Only one left-handed subject appeared with consistently left mirroring, while 22 right-handers mirrored with
the right hand. Since the Van Riper Test is claimed to show up
right-hand writers who are really left dominant, such a result

[1] The total mirroring at all angles on all four diagrams was used to
calculate these frequencies, those whose total was less with the right hand
being ranked as right dominant, whose total was less with the left hand as
left dominant, and equal as 'Ambi'.

TABLE XIX

DETAILS OF CONSISTENCY OF MIRRORING ON VAN RIPER TEST WITH
FOUR DIAGRAMS (ALL SUBJECTS)

	With Right Hand Only	With Left Hand First	With Right Hand Only	With Left Hand First	With Neither Hand	With Both Hands	Total
Right-Hand Writers							
Boys	6	4	32	13	3	92	150
Girls	8	4	47	20	1	82	162
Total	22		116		4	174	312
Left-Hand Writers							
Boys	5	1	–	1	–	5	12
Girls	1	–	–	–	–	5	6
Total	7		1			10	18

Number of Subjects Mirroring

might be understandable. However, the fact that 174 right-handed and 10 left-handed subjects (more than half the total group in each instance) mirrored with a different hand on different diagrams, is more difficult to explain, since, even should the indications of left tendencies in the 22 subjects mirroring with the right hand be accurate, the test is severely limited in its application if it cannot differentiate at all in half the cases.

A comparison was made of the distribution of mirroring in boys and girls in the group of right-hand writers. It may be seen from Table XIX that 102 boys and 94 girls mirrored with either the right hand or both hands, while 48 boys and 68 girls mirrored with the left hand or neither hand. The difference between the percentage of boys and girls mirroring with the writing hand was 10 per cent (S E of diff, 5·4). This sex difference in distribution among the right-hand writers was significant at the five per cent level of significance, indicating a greater tendency among boys than among girls to mirror with the writing hand.

II ANALYSIS OF INCONSISTENT RESULTS

A further analysis was made of the right-handed subjects

whose results were inconsistent on the four diagrams in order
to ascertain whether this inconsistency resulted from one diagram in particular or whether it was distributed throughout the
diagrams, in other words, to determine whether the exclusion
of any one of the diagrams would have increased the consistency
of the results. This analysis revealed that in 50 of the subjects
the inconsistency did not depend on one of the tests only. The
results of 6 of the subjects were excluded from the further
analysis because they had mirrored in only two of the four
diagrams. The remainder of the 174 subjects were consistent
in their mirroring on three of the diagrams. The greatest inconsistency resulted from Diagrams 1 and 4, while the remaining two diagrams, Diagram 2 and 3, were almost equal in the
amount of inconsistency they contributed. It was consequently
concluded that the exclusion of any one of the diagrams would
not have greatly increased the consistency of the results. Details of the actual mirroring on all four diagrams are set out in
Table XX from which it is apparent that Diagram 3 was most

TABLE XX

COMPARISON OF MIRRORING ON THE VAN RIPER TEST WITH DIFFERENT DIAGRAMS (ALL SUBJECTS)

| | Number of Subjects Mirroring | | | | |
	With Right Hand only	With Left Hand only	With Both Hands	With Neither Hand	Total
Right-Hand Writers					
Diagram 1	128	134	27	23	312
2	37	185	55	35	312
3	89	142	58	23	312
4	59	190	48	15	312
Left-Hand Writers					
Diagram 1	11	5	1	1	18
2	8	4	5	–	18
3	15	–	3	–	18
4	7	7	3	–	18

accurate in indicating the dominance of the left-handed subjects, where 15 mirrored with the right hand and 3 with
different hands at different angles. Considering the right-hand

subjects, almost equal numbers mirrored with the right and left hand on Diagram 1 (128 and 124 respectively). This diagram, which was used by Smith, and which was included because it was simple in design and yet asymmetrical, appears to have favoured right mirroring. One explanation of this may well be its resemblance to the numeral 'four' in reverse, a resemblance which seemed to strike, and possibly confuse, some of the subjects when attempting to draw it, several referring to it as 'the four'. This tendency to associate a diagram with some known symbol possibly operates in any test such as this, and it is probably impossible to devise any simple pattern which is asymmetrical and therefore serves the purposes of this test, and which yet does not bear a resemblance to some letter or numeral, either written normally or in reverse. The second diagram, the auditory stimulus 'three', also used by Smith, revealed a greater proportion of left- to right-hand mirroring than the other diagrams (185:37); this might be expected, since the bias in favour of the writing hand would be considerable in such a situation. Diagram 3 was one used by Van Riper, while Diagram 4 was the same figure in reverse. These were both included because it was felt that there might be something in the shape of the figure favouring the right or left hand. A few subjects were found with a tendency to draw the same double image throughout the testing no matter which was the stimulus, with the result that they were mirroring with the right hand in the first part and the left hand in the second. It might have been better, however, if these two diagrams had been separated in the testing, as in one or two instances there was a carry-over from Diagram 3 to the first attempt at Diagram 4, resulting in an appearance of inconsistency. It seems, nevertheless, that there is the possibility of a tendency, even with more complicated patterns, to prefer one double image to the other, or rather for one to be easier to perform with both hands at the same time, which may well be another complicating factor.

III DOMINANCE AS MEASURED BY THE VAN RIPER TEST

Any value which the Van Riper Test may have will depend on its ability to pick out left-handers who cannot be adequately differentiated by any other means. Thus the first step in analysing its effectiveness as a measure of dominance would seem to be a study of the results on the test of known left-handers, followed by a study of other aspects of those who, though not in fact left-hand writers, appear as left dominant on the basis of the Van Riper Test. In other words, do left-handers mirror with the right hand consistently on this test, and does consistent mirroring with the right hand in right-hand writers in fact indicate left dominance? Unless at least the first of these questions is answered in the affirmative, it is not justifiable to place any value on the test as a measure of laterality as generally defined, nor to place any significance on the right-hand mirroring of other right-hand writers.

A comparison was made between the results on each diagram of the left-hand writers and those of 14 right-hand writers who were found in the course of the rest of the study either to have had a preference for writing with the left hand but to have been changed over to the right, or to prefer the left hand in most other activities except writing. Left-hand writers would be expected to give more extreme results than the other left-handers, which was in fact the case. The contrast between the two groups was most pronounced in Diagram 2 which involved writing a figure for which the members of the second group were accustomed to use the right hand. The results of Diagram 3 are interesting since in this diagram, which was less connected with previous writing experiences than Diagram 2, the frequency of mirroring with the right hand was increased in the second group from one out of fourteen to eight out of fourteen subjects. There was therefore a tendency for left-handers, whether left-hand writers or changed left-handers, to mirror with the right hand rather than the left. Though this was by no means absolute, it was clearest in Diagram 3.

It may be seen from Table XIX that 22 right-hand writers showed left dominance as measured by the criterion of the Van Riper Test, namely, mirroring in all diagrams with the right hand. The results of these subjects on the other tests were analysed. The Simultaneous Writing Test, that most closely parallel to the Van Riper Test, showed eight subjects mirroring with the right hand only. Not one of these subjects mirrored with the right only in the Van Riper Test. Of the 22 subjects already mentioned as mirroring with the right, nine mirrored with the left only on the Simultaneous Writing Test, nine mirrored with neither, and four with both hands. One of the 22 was left-handed in all else but writing; three subjects showed some left preference in screwing, one in reaching, and two in throwing. In no other case was there any evidence of left preference. The indices of handedness obtained by this group on the Speed of Crossing Test ranged from 1·15 to 1·75, four scoring below 1·39, and a total of fourteen below, and six above the mean index for all right-hand writers of their own sex. The conclusion must be drawn that consistent right mirroring on the Van Riper Test did not have much connection with either a tendency to prefer the left hand or a narrow margin of ability between the two hands. In short there was little evidence of other left tendencies in those right-hand writers who consistently mirrored with the right hand on the Van Riper Test.

IV Comparison with the Simultaneous Writing Test

For comparisons the results obtained on the Van Riper Test and the Simultaneous Writing Test discussed earlier in the chapter are presented in Table XXI. It is evident from the table that there was no exact correspondence between the results of the two tests. More mirroring was, of course, apparent on the Van Riper Test where the task was more difficult and the distraction such as would increase the amount of mirroring. In the Simultaneous Writing Test there were 101 subjects who did not mirror with either hand, while on the other test there were only 4 subjects who mirrored with neither hand, these four who had no mirroring on the Van Riper Test had no mirroring on the Simultaneous Writing Test. When those who did not mirror on the Simultaneous Writing Test (101 subjects) are omitted from the comparison, the results of the two tests agreed in less than half of the remaining cases (92 out of 211 subjects). Of the 160 subjects who mirrored with the left hand only on the Simultaneous Writing Test, 66 mirrored with the left hand only and 94 with the right hand or both hands on the Van Riper Test; while of the 51 subjects who mirrored with the right or

TABLE XXI

COMPARISON OF FREQUENCY DISTRIBUTION ON VAN RIPER AND SIMULTANEOUS WRITING TESTS (RIGHT-HAND WRITERS)

No of Subjects Mirroring on Van Riper Test	Number of Subjects Mirroring on Simultaneous Writing Test[1]				
	With RH	With LH	With Both	With Neither	Total
With Right Hand	–	9	4	9	22
With Left Hand	1	66	13	32	112
With Both Hands	7	85	26	56	174
With Neither	–	–	–	4	4
Total	8	160	43	101	312

both on the Simultaneous Writing Test 37 subjects mirrored with the right hand or both on the Van Riper Test and 14 with the left hand. In short, mirroring with the writing hand on the simpler test did not necessarily mean a subject would mirror with that hand on the other test, and even less did mirroring with the non-writing hand on the simpler test mean that a subject would not mirror with the writing hand when the distraction was increased. A comparison was made between the Simultaneous Writing Test and the Van Riper Test, excluding those who mirrored with neither hand on the former test. On the basis of a fourfold table contrasting those who mirrored with the non-writing hand only and those who mirrored with the right hand or both hands, that is, with the writing hand, little connection between the two tests was found (χ^2 3·18, P ·10, ϕ ·22 max ϕ ·7).

V INTELLIGENCE AND TOTAL MIRRORING

The whole basis for the use of the Critical Angle Board as a measure of laterality, rather than two vertical boards placed back to back, is the claim of Van Riper that thereby it may be possible to take the angle at which mirroring occurs as a measure of degree of dominance. Van Riper dismissed the question of intelligence as unimportant; in fact, unless it is unimportant,

[1] Right mirroring includes all subjects mirroring with right consistently on all four diagrams and also all mirroring first with the right on each diagram—similarly with left. 'Both'—indicates inconsistency on different diagrams.

the whole basis of use of a certain angle as any measure of dominance is defeated. During the course of the present testing, it seemed that, even among subjects who were of approximately the same chronological age, and capable of drawing the more elaborate diagram fairly accurately, variations in intelligence were having some effect on the degree of mirroring produced. No matter at what speed the subjects were required to perform the task, a highly intelligent subject appeared to be able to prevent or delay mirroring, whereas mirroring seemed more frequent with the duller or more naive subject. To assess the truth of this impression and examine the extent of distortion of the results from such causes, a comparison was made between the intelligence of the subjects and the total mirroring they produced in the course of this test on all diagrams and at all

TABLE XXII

SCATTERGRAM SHOWING RELATIONSHIP BETWEEN INTELLIGENCE AND AMOUNT OF MIRRORING ON THE VAN RIPER TEST (RIGHT-HANDED SUBJECTS)

		INTELLIGENCE QUOTIENT[1]															
		70–74	75–79	80–84	85–89	90–94	95–99	100–104	105–109	110–114	115–119	120–124	125–129	130–134	135–139	140–144	Total
Total Mirroring On Van Riper Test	16	1			1	-	1	-	2	2							7
	15		1	2	-	1	-	1				1					6
	14					2	2	-	1								5
	13	1	-	1	1	2	4	2	-	2	2	1					16
	12			1	1	1	-	6	3	-	-	1					13
	11			1	-	1	2	3	4	-	1						12
	10		1	1	-	3	1	4	2	2	2	-	2				18
	9					5	5	9	4	5	2	1	1	1	1	1	35
	8			1	-	-	-	2	3	6	2	2	3	1	2	1	23
	7				7	1	7	2	4	5	8	3	2	-	1		40
	6		1	-	2	1	4	9	7	6	3	3	-	1	-	1	38
	5			1	2	2	5	7	4	3	7	7	-	2			40
	4				2	-	3	4	2	5	3	2	1	2	-	1	25
	3		1	-	-	-	-	1	1	2	2	3	1	2	1		14
	2						1	-	-	2	3	3	-	3	-	1	13
	1											1					1
	0							1	-	-	1	-	1	1			4
Total		2	3	6	16	14	34	47	41	42	35	29	15	13	8	5	310

[1] I Q was not available for two of the subjects who were therefore omitted from the table—hence 310 instead of 312 subjects

angles irrespective of the hand with which the mirroring was produced. The Intelligence Quotient used for the comparison was that secured in the course of the testing for the Primary Promotion Scheme, and was based on a written group intelligence test. The details of the comparison are set out in Table XXII, where the range in mirroring is from 0 to 16, zero indicating no mirroring on any diagram, and 16 standing for mirroring on all diagrams at all angles. It is at once apparent from the table that there is some correlation between the two variables, since no subject with an I Q of over 125 mirrored more than ten times, and at the other extreme, no subject with an I Q of less than 95 mirrored fewer than three times and only three fewer than five times. A calculation was made of the product-moment correlation between the two variables. This correlation was significant ($r = \cdot38$, S E$_r$ $\cdot049$). The inference is that the higher a subject's I Q the less mirroring he was likely to produce, a finding which makes the results unreliable as a measure of degree of dominance, and which would seem to indicate that as much might be discovered by the use of a simpler apparatus of two fixed vertical boards.

VI CRITICISMS

The following criticisms of the Van Riper Test are based on the experience gained in this present study of 330 children:

1 Individual testing is required, and a thorough testing as detailed by Van Riper is lengthy and very tiring for both subject and tester.

2 A single diagram is not sufficient for testing different subjects, since, if the diagram is too easy, no mirroring will take place and the subject will be classed as ambidextrous, but if the diagram is too difficult the actual reproduction may be so distorted that the mirroring is not distinguishable.

3 The actual scoring of the test is somewhat subjective. It is not always easy to determine whether a certain performance should be termed mirroring or not. Partial mirroring may take place very early, or the first mistake may be complete reversal. This complication becomes progressively apparent as the diagrams increase in difficulty.

4 The maturity of the subject affects the stage at which

mirroring takes place. Van Riper pointed out that some factor other than intelligence and attention was responsible for mirroring at a certain angle. It is clear, nevertheless, that intelligence does have some effect. Van Riper found that working the experiment in the reverse direction (ie from mirroring to nonmirroring), gave great inconsistency in the results and did not differentiate between the various laterality groups; this indicates that intelligence was probably a factor in the performance on the Critical Angle Board at the difficult position, awareness of mirroring possibly being of assistance in its prevention. The effect of intelligence on the performance is probably reduced when the test starts from the easier position, but it is certainly not eliminated. Further, its effect may vary with different degrees of laterality preference. A more intelligent subject may realise that, for example, the left hand is mirroring, and in concentrating on that hand at the next trial in an attempt to prevent this may well mirror with the right hand. This alternative mirroring does take place with some subjects, and conscious or subconscious awareness of the mirroring is the most likely explanation, suggesting that the testing is more effective with the more naive subjects. Further, Van Riper himself found that the critical angle does not remain constant even for one individual, but increases on retest, in other words, test sophistication results in an apparent decrease in the strength of a subject's hand dominance.

5 Such factors as the position of the experimenter may have some influence on the results. If, for example, he stands to the right, this may make the subject attend to that hand and hence mirror with the left. Van Riper tried control tests on a group of right- and left-handed subjects to determine the effect of such factors as attention, position of the hands and type of pattern. He found that the dominant hand mirrored in only four of thirty-one subjects. This ratio is too high, however, to entitle one to neglect such factors altogether.

6 The results of the present study confirm those of Smith[1] who found a considerable amount of right mirroring among right-handed subjects and many of her subjects not consistent at later angles. Since she was concerned with a comparison of

[1] *Loc cit*

the results obtained by a group of retarded readers and a group of reading achievers, and since, further, all her subjects were boys, it was not possible to make a full comparison in her study. She did not actually estimate laterality from the test, but made a comparison of the significance of the differences in results in the two groups. Her results do reveal, however, that an estimate of laterality with any certainty would have been as difficult in her study as it was in the present one.

7 There was considerable disagreement in the results on the different diagrams, and this disagreement could not be traced to any one diagram. It would be difficult to discover any diagram which would not in some way predispose to either left- or right-hand mirroring, since to serve the purpose of the experiment the diagram must be asymmetrical.

8 Those subjects who were right-hand writers and yet showed consistent right mirroring on all the diagrams, when their results were analysed and other information about them considered, were found to show little in the way of other left tendencies.

9 The results of the Van Riper Test were not in complete agreement with the simpler but similar Simultaneous Writing Test where the writing was also bimanual but horizontal.

It must be concluded that the Van Riper Test in its present form does not justify consideration as a single test or even inclusion in a battery of tests for diagnosing hand dominance, because of its unwieldiness, the difficulty of marking and interpreting the results, and the insufficient evidence that mirroring with one hand or the other has a precise connection with hand dominance. It does appear, nevertheless, that there is a tendency for left-handers to exhibit mirroring with the right hand, and for right-handers, though to a less degree, to show a tendency to mirror with the left hand. Agreement with Van Riper, however, that attention and intelligence are not sufficient to account for mirroring with a certain hand and at a certain angle, does not exclude the possibility that this mirroring has not a direct connection with hand dominance as generally interpreted. It is significant that though many clinics both in Britain and America have among their stock of apparatus a Critical Angle Board, few use it, and that, further, since his early studies in 1933 and 1934 Van Riper appears to have abandoned the apparatus in spite of his claims for its possibilities. In his Speech Clinic he apparently used a modified vertical board, and *not* a Critical Angle Board.[1] It may be that the use of the boards at only the most difficult position may reduce the influence of intelligence on the results as the subjects will then have less time in which to become aware of what is actually happening. It seems, therefore, that further research might most profitably be directed to ascertaining whether any reliable information may be obtained from a simpler form of apparatus, without the added complication of the movable boards. To be of value such a test would require first to pick out all left-hand writers (a few exceptions might be accounted for on the grounds of a person having developed left-hand usage though not left dominance because of, say, an accident or perversity). Further, it would have to be shown that it could pick out accurately those with left tendencies among right-hand writers. Only then could a test on these lines be considered of other than academic interest as a measure of laterality preference. It is possible, however, that extensive mirroring with the writing hand when found in children above a certain age, and especially in those not of low intelligence, may have some educational significance. There still remain many unanswered questions on the meaning of mirroring found on a test such as this; why even in designs unconnected with writing there should be a tendency for the non-writing hand to mirror; what explains the sex difference in the mirroring with the writing hand; and why, as Smith found, poorer readers tend to mirror more frequently with the writing hand. All these and many other problems will have to await further research for their solution.

[1] C Van Riper, *Speech Correction, Principles and Methods*, pp 292-294

CHAPTER XIX

RESULTS OF THE WRITING TEST

GENERAL DISCUSSION

THE Writing Test performed by each subject was given as a group test, the passage to be written being learnt beforehand, then written as quickly and as well as possible for the two minutes of the test. Two practice attempts were given which were not scored, then a final scored trial. The preliminary attempts were found necessary since instructions, no matter how simple, are never followed exactly by a complete class of over forty children, and failure to do so would upset the results. The most common error was for a child to stop writing when he had completed the passage once, instead of writing it again and again until the two minutes were over. This sort of mistake was, however, easily corrected during the practice trials. The testing of each class was made as nearly identical as possible, while absentees were tested individually or in groups under similar conditions.

The material to be written was learnt before the test so that the child might concentrate on the writing, and in order that speed might be measured without the distraction present when material is copied. The aim of the Paul West Test used in this study was to make possible the measurement of both speed and quality at the same time. Possibly it is difficult, or even impossible, to measure both these factors adequately within the bounds of one test. However, from the limited point of view of the present study, where the concern is the effect of left-handedness on writing rather than a study of writing *per se*, this test seemed suitable, especially since it was particularly desired to study the effects of left-handedness under conditions as near to normal as possible.

The test papers revealed that speed could be measured without much difficulty but that quality would be very difficult to estimate, particularly since the Paul West norms for American children were not suitable for use with Scottish children who have a totally different style of writing. A preliminary study of the scripts revealed that the greatest factor in determining the quality of writing appeared to be the teacher or teachers under whom the children had studied, the stamp of the individual teacher appearing in all eight groups of scripts. Writing is, of course, a subject where the range of interest of teachers is considerable, and therefore the time and attention devoted to that subject will vary considerably, even within the bounds of apparently similar curricula. Since only one, or sometimes two, left-handers customarily appear in any one class, the dangers of comparing a group of left-handers with right-handers, unless they are from the same class, are apparent. Further, since boys are usually recognised as on the average poorer writers than girls, and there are more boys than girls who write with the left hand, it is further necessary to ensure that the left-handers are compared with right-handers of the same sex. The aim here was to estimate not the absolute ability of left-handers in writing but rather the effect on writing of performing it with the left hand rather than the right, and more particularly to ascertain how true it is that left-hand writers are slower and/or poorer writers than those who use the right hand; another main aim was to ascertain how others who, though right-hand writers, had left-hand tendencies compared with right-hand writers who had not such tendencies.

The speed scores in the Writing Test will be discussed first, and will then be compared with the results of the Speed of Crossing Test. Finally the quality of the writing will be discussed.

SPEED OF WRITING

Speed of writing was calculated from the number of letters written in two minutes. Incomplete letters were counted if they were recognisable. The results obtained here were considerably below the speeds given in the norms supplied by West for American children. However, it is generally recognised that the writing of British children is in fact slower than that of American children, since the emphasis in the teaching in the United States is on movement rather than on form, whereas in

N

Britain the emphasis is on form at the expense of speed. The mean score for the girls was slightly higher than that for the boys (107·9, 104·8) and the standard deviation slightly greater (28·4, 25·4). The difference between the means was not, however, enough to be significant. Of the eighteen left-hand writers eight boys and one girl scored above the mean for right-hand writers of their own sex, while four boys and five girls scored below the corresponding mean for right-handers. Since the left-hand writers were not evenly distributed in the eight classes used in the testing, and since there were considerable differences in speed of writing in the different classes, the actual scores of left-hand writers are presented in Table XXIII, along with the mean and range in the class to which they belonged.

TABLE XXIII

SPEED SCORES OF LEFT-HAND WRITERS ON WRITING TEST RELATIVE TO RIGHT-HAND WRITERS IN OWN CLASS

		Right-Hand Writers		Left-Hand Writers	
School	Number	Mean Score	Range of Scores	Number	Actual Scores
A1	38	119	77–192	3	119, 128, 138
A2	46	102·7	55–151	1	69
B1	38	117·8	69–172	1	124
B2	46	101·7	54–175	2	93, 107
B3	38	112·8	50–155	1	136
B4	38	90·6	61–137	2	80, 95
C1	35	118·1	58–176	3	51, 75, 101
C2	33	112·8	70–162	5	88, 89, 113 113, 120

An attempt at a more precise study of the left-hand writers as compared with right-hand writers was made, and to that end, each left-hander was paired with a right-hand writer in the same class, of the same sex, and with the same intelligence quotient. A similar paired group was established of fourteen right-hand writers who were either changed left-handers or had strong left-hand tendencies, paired for sex, class and I Q with right-hand writers with no apparent left-hand tendencies. In both paired groups it was possible in nearly all instances to find a mate for each left-hand writer or subject with left-hand tendencies whose intelligence quotient was almost identical with his. The mean I Q of the left-hand writers was 108·7 and of the paired right-handers 109, and the greatest single difference between the I Qs of any pair was nine points. The mean I Q for the right-hand writers with left-hand tendencies was 106·5 and of the paired right-handers it was 107·6, and the greatest single difference was ten points of I Q. In the few instances where there were two right-handed subjects with the same I Q as the left-hander, in the same class and of the same sex, then the first on the alphabetical list of subjects was selected; this occurrence was, however, rare.

The results of the comparison of speed of writing in these two paired groups are shown in Table XXIV, where it may be seen that the means for both the left-hand writers and for those

TABLE XXIV

PAIRED COMPARISON OF LEFT- AND RIGHT-HANDERS
ON SPEED OF WRITING

	Left-Hand Writers		Subjects with Left-Hand Tendencies	
	Left-Handers	Paired Right-Handers	Left-Handers	Paired Right-Handers
Number of Subjects	18	18	14	14
Mean Speed	102·2	108·7	104·4	115·1
Standard Deviation of Scores	23·4	17·3	29·8	23·8
Difference Between the Means		6·5		10·7
Standard Error of the Difference		5·6		9·3

with left-hand tendencies are lower than the corresponding means for the paired right-handers, and that in both groups the standard deviation is greater in the left-handed group. A study was made of the differences between the means, the differences being 6·5 and 10·7 respectively for the left-hand writers and those with left-hand tendencies. The correlations in the two paired groups of scores were calculated in order to correct the standard errors of the differences for paired samples. The Standard Errors of the differences were 5·6 and 9·3 respectively, thus neither of the differences was significant. The results of this study do not, therefore, support the hypothesis that left-handers are slower writers than right-handers of the same sex and intelligence, taught in the same class, though the small numbers used in this test would prevent one from asserting that this is always the position with all left-handers.

COMPARISON OF SPEED ON THE WRITING AND CROSSING TESTS

The results of the Speed of Crossing Test are set out in detail in Chapter XVII. A comparison was made between the results of that test, where speed only was emphasised and the task was to draw a series of crosses as quickly as possible, and the Writing Test, where words had to be written and quality and speed were both emphasised. The emphasis on quality in the Writing Test reduced the average quantity produced. Whereas in the Writing Test the average numbers of letters per minute were 52·4 and 54 for boys and girls respectively, the average numbers of crosses per minute were 83·4 and 92·4 respectively. Thus, the actual amount produced was reduced in the Writing Test, as also was the ratio of the girls' scores to those of the boys. Though the girls still scored slightly better than the boys in the Writing Test, the difference between the means was not significant in that test, whereas in the Crossing Test it was. The implication would seem to be that the absolute ability of the girls in a task such as this is better than the boys as far as speed only is concerned but that the necessity to concentrate also on quality reduces that superiority.

The correlations between the scores of the right-handed subjects on the two tests were calculated for boys and girls separately and indicated some relationship between the two tests. The correlation between the boys' scores on the two tests was slightly higher than that between the girls' scores (r ·46, S E$_r$ ·06 for the boys and r ·35, S E$_r$ ·07 for the girls) but the Z test applied to the difference between the two correlations[1] indicated that this

[1] Garrett, *op cit*, pp 239-240

difference was not significant. The actual scores on each test of the left-hand writers and those with left-hand tendencies were compared with the mean of the right-handers of the same sex. The results are shown in Table XXV, eight left-hand writers and six with left-hand tendencies scoring below the mean on both tests, while three and four respectively scored above the mean on both tests, most of the others were above the mean on the Writing Test but below in the Crossing Test.

TABLE XXV

COMPARISON OF LEFT-HANDERS WITH MEAN OF RIGHT-HANDERS OF THE SAME SEX ON WRITING AND SPEED OF CROSSING TEST

			Crossing Test				
			Boys		*Girls*		
			Above Mean	*Below Mean*	*Above Mean*	*Below Mean*	*Total*
Writing Test	Group *L H*	Above Mean	2	6	1	0	9
		Below Mean	0	4	1	4	9
		Total	2	10	2	4	18
	Group *l h*	Above Mean	1	0	3	3	7
		Below Mean	1	3	0	3	7
		Total	2	3	3	6	14

L H Left-Hand Writers
l h Right-Hand Writers with Left-Hand Tendencies

QUALITY OF WRITING

In view of the considerable disagreement between observers generally in any estimates of quality of handwriting, and in particular the lack of consistency when, in the present study, observers were asked to rank the eighteen scripts from the left-hand writers, it seemed a formidable task to attempt to get all 330 scripts marked for quality of handwriting with anything approaching consistency in marking. Since it was felt that little extra reliable information pertinent to the aspect of handwriting here under consideration was to be gained from a study of the quality of writing in the total group, attention was confined to the paired groups discussed in an earlier section of this chapter. The writing scripts belonging to the eighteen paired left- and right-handers, and the fourteen pairs of subjects with and without left-hand tendencies, were singled out. The actual sample of writing was on one side of the paper, and the name of the pupil, his school and class were on the back, leaving no distinguishing mark evident to the observers which would differentiate the two scripts of each pair. Thus the pairs of subjects were matched for class, sex and intelligence, while one of each pair had either left-hand tendencies or wrote with the left hand, the other writing with the right hand. Each pair of scripts was given a key letter, the first group being numbered from 'A' to 'R', and the second group (containing those with left-hand tendencies) from 'a' to 'n'. Each pair of scripts was shown in turn to a series of seven observers who were asked to decide which of the two scripts was the *better* writing—by their criterion. The seven observers studied all the scripts in this way, not aware that one of each pair in the first set had been written with the left hand. From these estimates a table was then prepared showing whether the left-hander of each pair was considered better or worse than the right-hander. Finally, the first eighteen pairs of scripts, where one was actually written with the left hand and one with the right, were again shown to the observers who were this time told that one of each pair was left-handed and were asked to determine which of the pair it was.

Considerable consistency in estimates of quality was found among the seven observers when the method just described was employed, and it was possible in most instances to determine which of each pair of scripts was generally considered the better writing. If five or more observers were agreed that the writing was better or worse, then that decision was accepted; if there was less agreement than that, it was assumed that there was little difference in quality between the two samples in the pair, and they were therefore classed as 'doubtful'. Seven left-hand writers were judged worse than the right-handers, nine were judged better and two 'doubtful', while the parallel results for those with left-hand tendencies as compared with the right-handers were five worse, four better and five 'doubtful'. Thus, though there were left-handers better or worse than the right-handers there was no apparent tendency for the left-handers generally to be either worse or better than the right-handers so far as was indicated by the results of this study.

The ability of the seven observers to recognise the writing of the left-handers was then studied in order to determine whether they tended to rate as worse that writing which was easily distinguished as having been written with the left hand. The ability to recognise the writing of the left-handers ranged from 15 out of 18 for one observer (himself left-handed) to 6 out of 18. Table XXVI shows, for the seven observers, details of their judgments on the writing of the left-handers, as compared with the right-handers, and also their ability to distinguish the writing which had been performed with the left hand. The results show that 70 per cent of those judged as worse were recognised as left-handed and 61 per cent of those judged as better were recognised. The ease with which the writing was recognised as left-hand writing seemed to bear little relation to the observers' judgments as to its relative quality, except possibly in the case of the first observer who recognised only six of the scripts of left-handers, less than chance expectation, and all six scripts were ones which he had already judged as poorer.

TABLE XXVI

COMPARISON BETWEEN ABILITY TO RECOGNISE LEFT-HAND WRITING
AND ESTIMATE OF ITS QUALITY (SEVEN JUDGES)

Number of Scripts of Left-Handers

| | Judged Worse | | Judged Better | |
Judges	Total	Recognised as L H	Total	Recognised as L H
1	12	6	6	–
2	8	7	10	8
3	11	7	7	6
4	10	9	8	4
5	8	7	10	7
6	9	5	9	7
7	9	6	9	4
Total	67	47	59	36
Mean	9·6	6·7	8·4	5·1

COMPARISON BETWEEN QUALITY AND SPEED OF WRITING

Four of the left-handers were both quicker and better in writing than their paired right-handers, three were slower and worse. Left-handers did not, more than right-handers, appear to sacrifice quality to speed or speed to quality.

When the results of right-hand writers with left-hand tendencies were considered it was found that one of this group was better and quicker than the right-handed partner, and only one was slower and worse, while three were slower but better and four worse but quicker. There seemed in this group a slight tendency to be either worse or slower, but not both. Unfortunately this group which was already small, having only fourteen pairs, was further reduced for purpose of comparison by the fact that the judges here were in disagreement in more instances with regard to quality. Possibly the very fact that the two members of each pair in the other group wrote with different hands in some way facilitated the comparisons of quality, making them more uniform. The greater than chance accuracy with which the observers could recognise the writing of the left-handers would indicate that in many cases it did have some distinguishing features.

The left-handers and those with left-hand tendencies were in this test of writing distributed evenly above and below the mean for right-handers of the same sex. When a further study was made of matched groups it was found that there was no tendency for the left-handers to be significantly poorer than the right-handers of the same sex, class and intelligence, either with regard to speed or quality of writing. With such a small number of subjects, however, it would be more correct to conclude that if such a tendency does exist, an investigation on a much larger scale than the present one would be required to confirm it.

CHAPTER XX

ANALYSIS OF THE RESULTS OF THE LEFT-HANDED SUBJECTS

IN THE preceding chapters attention has been concentrated on the findings on the total group of subjects, though reference has been made incidentally to the left-hand writers. This present chapter will, however, be devoted to a more detailed analysis of the left-handed subjects, both those writing with the left hand, and those who showed left-hand tendencies. Their results in the battery of tests of the various laterality characteristics will be discussed and a comparison made between their achievement marks in the Promotion Examination and those of their right-handed fellows.

ANALYSIS OF THE PREFERENCE TEST RESULTS

The group of eighteen left-hand writers in the present study might justifiably be assumed to be extreme left-handers, since they use that hand for writing, yet it was found in this present study, as previous investigators have suggested, that they were not, in fact, as complete in their left-hand preferences as were some of the right-handed subjects in their preference for their right hand. Even in the tests of hand preference, only seven of the left-hand writers showed left preference on each trial of each test, three of the boys showing preference for the right hand in throwing. In the tests of eye preference nine subjects showed left preference on all trials of all four tests, for six subjects there was not agreement on all the tests, while the remaining three were right-eyed in all four tests, a result in contrast to that found in the total group of 330 subjects, where the frequencies were 48·5 per cent right-eyed, 25·5 per cent doubtful, and 26 per cent left-eyed.

The preference test results for the fourteen subjects with left-hand tendencies revealed that while five of them showed right preference on all three trials of the tests of hand preference, the remaining nine showed disagreement on the tests, in other words, showed some left tendency. It is worth noting that of the five who showed right preference in all three tests, four were right-eyed on all four tests of eyedness. One of these claimed only to deal cards with the left hand, the other three who were right-eyed and right-handed on the preference tests had actually been left-hand writers at some time, but had changed or been changed to the right hand. It would appear that in these instances the change had been complete. A further point of interest is the finding that of the total group of fourteen with left-hand tendencies, only four now use the left hand for anything actually connected with writing—three for drawing and ruling lines, while the fourth writes with either, but usually the right—and these are the only four left-eyed on all four tests of eyedness. Though final conclusions on this matter cannot be drawn from so small a group, it does, nevertheless, indicate various lines of possible research—to ascertain whether transfer to right-handedness is only complete or more likely to be complete in those not left-eyed, whether subjects who are both left-handed and left-eyed are more extreme cases of left laterality, or as a third alternative, whether a change of eye dominance may in fact take place in those who change over completely to right-handedness.

A further point to be noted is the contrast between eyedness in these two groups. Whereas among the left-hand writers there were three right-eyed, nine left-eyed and six inconsistent, in the group with only left-hand tendencies there were nine right-eyed, four left-eyed and one inconsistent.

FINE MOVEMENT AND ALTERNATING MOVEMENT TESTS

These tests which formed part of the battery have not yet been discussed, as it was decided in the course of the testing that the results obtained were not sufficiently objective to warrant inclusion as an important part of the study. Difficulties soon became apparent as they were being applied. Since, however, they only took a minute or two to apply it was decided to retain them in the battery on the chance that they might reveal some interesting material in individual instances. With regard to the Fine Movement Test, it was found that, in order to utilise such a method, a more elaborate experimental set-up would be required. In the present study, the child was asked to transfer a series of metal balls from a box into a small tube by means of a pair of tweezers, and a note was made of the hand used at the first attempt, and of the time taken to perform the task, which was then repeated with the other hand. Difficulties, such as the child dropping one of the balls, made effective timing of the action impossible; it was possible, however, to make a subjective estimate of the relative ability of the two hands. In the Alternating Movement Test it was found that some of the subjects were incapable of making their two hands rotate in alternating directions at the same time; others though capable of making the movement showed poor co-ordination with one hand; still others could make both hands function fairly well to start with, but one hand tired long before the other. An analysis of the results of the left-handers on this test revealed the following points of interest. In the Alternating Movement Test eight of the group of left-hand writers were much the same with both hands, five were poorer with the right, four were very poor with both hands, and the remaining subject could not do the test. In the group with left-hand tendencies, four were more or less the same with both hands, three were poor with both hands, and five and two respectively were poorer with the right and left hand. In the Fine Movement Test all the left-hand writers except two used the left hand first in the test, while five of those with left-hand tendencies used the left hand first, and the remaining nine used the right first.

ACHIEVEMENT TEST RESULTS AND LEFT-HANDEDNESS

The achievement test results of the total group of 330 subjects will not be discussed in any great detail, since they did not form part of the actual testing carried out in the course of the present study. It is necessary, however, to mention several points in connection with them preparatory to a comparison of left- and right-handers on these tests.

Both the Group Intelligence Test and the Achievement Test marks used in the study were those obtained in the course of the testing for allocation to secondary schools by the Glasgow

Education Committee. The Achievement Test mark used here was the sum of the scores on the Arithmetic and English Tests. The correlation between the results of the Intelligence Test and the Achievement Test marks was calculated by means of the Pearson product-moment correlation, yielding a correlation of r ·77, S E$_r$ ·03 for the right-handed boys and r ·74, S E$_r$ ·04 for the right-handed girls. The results of one boy and one girl had to be omitted as they were not on the schedule for the class, though they were in the class at the time this study took place. The mean I Q of the right-handed boys was 109·4 (S D 14·2) and of the right-handed girls 109·3 (S D 13·7); while the mean Achievement scores were 111·2 (S D 22·2) and 113·2 (S D 21·3) respectively.

The paired groups used in earlier sections of the study[1] were used again here to compare the left-hand writers with right-hand writers matched for sex, class and I Q, and to compare the right-hand writers with left-hand tendencies with right-hand writers without such tendencies. The mean Achievement mark of the left-hand writers was 111·6 (S D 19·8), and the corresponding mean for the paired right-handers was 115·6 (S D 17·0). The standard error of the difference was calculated, corrected for correlated samples, and found to be 3·3, thus the difference between the two means, 4·0, was not large enough to be significant. The group of left-hand writers did not accordingly score significantly lower than right-handers on the Achievement Tests. The mean Achievement mark of the right-handers with left-hand tendencies was found to be 97·5 (S D 30·2) and the corresponding mean for the paired right-handers was 110·3 (S D 16·0). The standard error of the difference between the two means, corrected for correlated samples, was 5·2, thus the difference between the means (12·8) was significant at the five per cent level of significance (t 2·46). The mean Achievement Score of the right-hand writers with left-hand tendencies was, in other words, significantly poorer than that of right-handers matched for sex, class and intelligence, but having no apparent left-hand tendencies. Those who were actual changed left-hand writers scored more than twenty points below the paired right-hander, and one as much as fifty points below.

[1] *Supra*, pp 176-9

It would be unjustifiable to draw any final conclusion from these small groups on the effects of left-handedness on achievement in school, or on the placing of those writing with the left hand relative to those who have been changed to right-handedness. As far as this study is concerned, it has been shown that whereas the left-hand writers were not poorer than the right-handers of the same sex, class and intelligence, those with left-hand tendencies were inclined to be so, and that the most glaring examples of this were in those who had actually been forced to use the right hand, even though all five of them were right-eyed. If these subjects were penalised in tests where little writing was involved, they may be even more so in studies where much writing is required since the use of an achievement test removes as far as this is possible the influence of speed and style of writing.

The other tests in the battery will not be discussed further here as the results of the left-handers in these were discussed in some detail in the relevant chapters. The section of this chapter which follows will be devoted to a discussion of the information gained from the left-handers during talks in the course of the testing.

INFORMATION ON LEFT-HANDEDNESS GAINED FROM THE LEFT-HANDED SUBJECTS

Most of the left-hand writers stated that they had at some time been encouraged or forced to attempt to write with the right hand—usually about the age of eight years. In several instances this occurred when the child changed to a different school, indicating that though the official policy is to permit left-handers to write with the left hand, there are teachers and schools which do not follow this practice. It is interesting to note that subject 'B' who was left-handed in all the preference tests, had never been made to try with her right hand, she said, because her mother had instructed the teacher to allow her to use the left hand, her mother being left-handed herself in most things except writing. Subject 'D' said that her mother had tried to change her before she started school, as she thought she was 'just putting it on'—it is worth noting that there was no instance of left-handedness among her close relatives. Subject

'F' stated that attempts were made to check her in the infant room at school, but that she could not use the right hand. More recently she has been reprimanded because her writing with her left hand has different slants. On being asked whether she had tried sloping the paper, she replied that she had, but had been told by the teacher to keep it straight. Subject 'I' was rather interesting because, when his position was discussed with the teacher, he claimed that the boy was not left-handed but only trying to be different. The fact that his preference results showed right preference in all the tests, where he did not realise that handedness was being tested, would lend support to this view. He admitted that when he broke his left arm he wrote with the right hand for a time, but when the left healed he returned to it. Apparently his parents had also attempted to force him to use the right hand, without success. It was observed that when he wrote in class, he turned the paper right round so that he wrote towards the body, and rather seemed to like being reprimanded for that.

Subject 'L' said that when he was six years old he was made to use his right hand and to put his left hand behind his back, but was so poor with his right hand that he was permitted to return to the left. He confessed that he had great difficulty in writing, and that the fine nib used in schools caused the ink to spurt and blot the writing, with the result that he was frequently punished for bad writing. Further, his hand was inclined to go numb when he did much writing. This was probably the result of the clenched position of his hand writing, which meant that he was straining the hand all the time. Subject 'M' said his mother had tried to change him, but never any of the teachers, although one teacher had said that she did not like left-handers.

In the group with left-hand tendencies, there was one subject, 'm' who was still writing with the left hand occasionally, and several ('b', 'c' and 'd') who used the left hand for drawing and ruling lines. Other subjects who had at one time written with the left hand and been changed over to the right were content to write with the right hand and use the left for other activities. One girl, 'f', said she had used her left for a few years but had changed to the right hand because she was not very good with her left; another girl, 'h', admitted that when she had used her left she had been corrected repeatedly for bad writing and was the only left-hander in the class, and that her mother had suggested that she should practise with the right hand—which she now uses for everything. One of the boys, 'n', said that when he started school he used his left hand, but was forced to use his right. He was taken away from that school because they had forced him to change to the right hand; he still uses the right hand for writing and is quite efficient with it.

These extracts from the information gained by questioning the left-handed subjects reveal the diversity of treatment to which they were subjected, not only varying from individual to individual, but also in one child as between home and school, or from teacher to teacher.

SEX DIFFERENCE IN HANDEDNESS

The sex difference in handedness as far as writing is concerned has already been discussed in connection with the inheritance of handedness.[1] It was there suggested that the sex difference might result from temperamental factors rather than from any actual difference in degree of native dominance. The finding in the present study of only six girls writing with the left hand and twelve boys using that hand for writing suggests a similar trend to that found by previous investigators, while the reverse trend was in fact noted in those with left-hand tendencies but not writing with the left hand, the numbers there being nine girls and five boys with left-hand tendencies, making the total numbers with any left tendencies more or less the same for the two sexes. In an attempt to estimate more accurately the actual percentages of boys and girls writing with the left hand, a form was sent to each teacher in the eight schools in which the testing took place, asking for information of the total number of boys and girls on the roll, the total number now using the left hand only for writing, and also particulars of any other children who had at some time used the left hand, and, if they had been changed to the right hand, by whom. It was realised that this latter part of the form would certainly be an under-estimation of the numbers involved, but it seemed worth asking for that

[1] *Supra*, pp 11-12, 15

information at the same time as that concerning present left-handers. The results are shown in Table XXVII where the figures obtained in the individual schools are listed separately. The percentage of left-handedness found in the three grades of school were 7·6, 6·7 and 6·9 per cent for above average, average and below average schools respectively. The differences between these percentages are not significant. The percentages of left-hand writers in the eight schools were 8 per cent of boys

TABLE XXVII

TOTAL NUMBERS OF LEFT-HAND WRITERS IN EACH OF THE EIGHT
PRIMARY SCHOOLS USED FOR TESTING

School	Number on Roll		Number of Left-hand Writers		Total on Roll	Total of Left-Hand Writers
	Boys	Girls	Boys	Girls		
A 1	471	478	40	24	949	64
A 2	415	409	41	30	824	71
B 1	447	434	37	27	881	64
B 2	249	236	25	19	485	44
B 3	411	380	19	21	791	40
B 4	450	412	35	18	862	53
C 1	233	246	13	12	479	25
C 2	269	250	26	18	519	44
Above A—Average	886	887	81	54	1773	135
B—Average	1557	1462	116	85	3019	201
Below C—Average	502	496	39	30	998	69
Totals	2945	2845	236	169	5790	405

and 5·9 per cent of girls. The difference between these percentages was significant, indicating a greater proportion of boys than girls using the left hand for writing, as was found in previous studies. In addition to the percentage found using the left hand only, another 1·2 per cent were reported as having used the left hand for writing at some time, and the majority of these were reported to have been changed at home rather than at school. Even if this is an accurate picture of the reason for changing, it does not necessarily mean that the school had no part in making the parent feel it would be better for the child to use the right rather than the left hand. The figure for left-handedness found here—approximately 7 per cent, using the left hand in writing, indicates a considerable increase in recent years in the amount of apparent left-handedness. Whether this is only an increase in apparent left-handedness, resulting from the more tolerant attitude, it is hard to say. Further, how representative these figures, obtained from almost six thousand children under the age of twelve, are for the rest of Scotland, and how they would compare with present-day figures from other countries cannot at present be determined. A further line of study would be an attempt to ascertain whether the incidence of left-handedness varies greatly in different districts, and whether it is constant in different age groups.[1]

In the course of the present study information was obtained from the subjects on left-handedness and twinning among their immediate relatives. Though lack of positive information could not be accepted as absence of any left-handedness in the family, it was fair to assume that the instances reported were accurate. In view, however, of the difficulty of gaining full information on the more distant relatives, the figures were calculated from only the siblings of the subjects who were tested. The results of that information may be seen in Table XXVIII. Since information on children of school age and over was likely to be more accurate than that on younger children, the data on children under five years of age were treated separately. A sex difference was again apparent in these results, and the total percentage of left-handers, 6·1, was slightly lower than that found for children between five and twelve, which could be accounted for by the presence in the group of siblings of some over school age.

[1] The Scottish Council for Research in Education carried out a survey on a complete age-group of 10-11 year old Scottish children in 1953. During the course of that testing the teachers were asked to observe whether the pupil wrote the tests with the left or right hand. The results of that investigation are given in the appendix. The percentages are comparable to those in Table XXVII. It should, however, be borne in mind that the percentages obtained during the present investigation are percentages of left-hand writers in the age-group 5 to 12 years of age, whereas the Research Council figures are based on a one-age-group sample. It is worth noting that the percentage of left-hand writers found in the Research Council survey was higher in the cities (a city also being used in the present investigation), and that it was highest of all in the private schools.

o

TABLE XXVIII
LEFT-HANDEDNESS AMONG SIBLINGS OF SUBJECTS TESTED[1]

Siblings	LH[2]	RH	Total	Percentage Left-Handed
Boys	22	287	309	7·1
Girls	14	264	278	5·0
All	36	551	587	6·1

Another 10 out of 116 siblings under the age of five years were reported as showing left-handed tendencies, but without actually seeing the children it was impossible to estimate what strength these tendencies had, as some parents would notice slight attempts to use the left hand, while others might remain unaware of even more pronounced attempts until the child attempted to use the left hand for writing.

Finally a study was made of the left-handedness and twinning among the relatives of the left-handed subjects. A summary of the data may be seen in Table XXIX. It is worth noting that

TABLE XXIX
DETAILS OF KNOWN LEFT-HANDEDNESS AND TWINNING AMONG THE RELATIVES OF LEFT-HANDERS

Number of Subjects with	Left-Hand Writers	Subjects with Left-Hand Tendencies
Left-Handedness and Twinning among relatives	0	2
Left-handedness only	10	6
Twinning only	2	1
Neither	6	5
Total	18	14

four of the left-hand writers and one of those with left-hand tendencies (who actually draws with the left hand) stated that their mother was left-handed, while none in either group had a left-handed father. This is particularly noteworthy in view of the finding that in the total group of 330 subjects approximately

[1] Only siblings of school age or over are included, i e, who have reached the age of five years
[2] All those reported as left-handed are included

equal numbers had left-handed fathers or mothers (16 and 17 respectively). There was little evidence of twinning in the left-handed groups, but the two instances which did occur among the left-hand writers were both cases of twins among the siblings. It would be presumptuous to attempt an analysis of the hereditary mechanism at work in the transmission of hand dominance on the basis of the information supplied by the children tested in this study, particularly in view of the difficulties which have been encountered by geneticists in their attempts to account for the phenomenon. The information was gathered here with the aim, rather, of studying the family background of left-handedness as one factor affecting the attitude to the individual left-hander.

CHAPTER XXI

SUMMARY AND CONCLUSIONS

SUMMARY

THE first part of the present study is a critical analysis of the main investigations which have been performed on the more important aspects of laterality characteristics, while the second part describes an investigation into the laterality characteristics of a group of 330 school children of about eleven years of age. The children (162 boys and 168 girls) were subjected to a battery of eighteen tests of the various aspects of lateral asymmetry and to a writing test. In addition, the marks obtained by the subjects on the Group Intelligence Test and the Achievement Tests, which are administered to all children in the schools under the Glasgow Education Committee on the completion of the Primary Stage of their education, were utilised in the present study. The following are the main findings of the experimental section of the study:

I PREFERENCE TESTS

Thirteen preference tests were performed by the subjects, three tests each of hand, foot and ear preferences, and four tests measuring eye preference. Four trials were given on each test.

1 Right preference predominated in all tests of preference, the greatest percentage of right preference being evident in the tests of handedness.

2 In the tests of hand preference, screwing and throwing were the two activities with the greatest correlation. Reaching, though positively correlated with the other two, showed more undecided subjects. The percentages for right, left and doubtful preference on all three tests were 71·5, 2·4 and 26·1 per cent respectively, taking all those not consistent on all twelve trials as 'doubtful'.

3 The foot preference tests of kicking and hopping were

positively correlated, but there was no significant connection between the foot used in stepping off and the foot used in the other two activities.

4 The two ear preference tests, Sound in Box and the Stop Watch Test, gave similar results, while the results of the Head Turning Test were connected with the former but not with the latter test.

5 There was a close connection between the results of all four tests of eyedness, the Cone, Hole in Card, Peep Show and Cylinder Tests. The percentages for right, left and doubtful preference were 48·5, 26 and 25·5 per cent respectively, taking all those who were not consistent on all sixteen trials as 'doubtful'.

6 A significant correlation was found between each of the three tests of hand preference and the Kicking Test of footedness, and also between the Hopping Test and both the Screwing and Throwing Tests of handedness.

7 The ear preferred in the Stop Watch Test of earedness, where the subject was permitted to hold the watch, had some connection with the hand preferred in the hand preference tests, as also had the direction in which the head was turned at a sound, while the results in the Sound in Box Test of earedness, where the direct influence of handedness was removed, were related to the preferred eye.

8 There was no relation between the preferred hand in the tests of hand preference and the preferred eye.

9 No connection was evident between those who were non-dominant or changeable in the tests of handedness and those who were doubtful on the tests of eyedness.

10 The boys showed a greater tendency than the girls towards left preference in all tests of hand, foot and ear preference (except the Hopping Test). However, only in reaching, stepping and the Stop Watch Test were the differences great enough to be significant.

II SPEED OF CROSSING TEST

The Speed of Crossing Test measured the relative ability of the writing and non-writing hand in drawing crosses at a high speed.

1 A sex difference was found in ability to perform the test, girls being on the average quicker than boys.

2 There was a tendency for the left-hand writers to be slower than right-handers of the same sex in performing the task with the writing hand.

3 The ratio of ability with the writing hand to ability with the non-writing hand was calculated, and showed that in the left-hand writers there was a tendency for the two hands to be closer in ability than were those of the right-hand writers.

4 A significantly smaller ratio of ability with the writing hand to that with the non-writing hand was found among the right-handed boys than among the right-handed girls, in other words, the superiority of the right hand over the left hand was greater among the girls.

5 A significantly greater percentage of those with a low index of handedness on this test showed some left tendencies on the preference tests than showed no such tendencies; while a greater percentage of those with a high index of handedness showed right preference on all the tests than showed any left tendency.

III SIMULTANEOUS WRITING TEST

1 When visual cues to direction were removed, as in this test, there was a tendency for the non-writing hand to mirror in bimanual writing; there was nevertheless some mirroring with the hand accustomed to writing. In the total group of subjects, the mirroring with the right hand was approximately one-sixth as frequent as mirroring with the left hand.

2 There was no evidence of mirroring in one-third of the subjects, while 45 subjects mirrored with both hands. All but eight of the remaining subjects mirrored with the writing hand only.

IV THE VAN RIPER TEST

Simultaneous drawing with both hands was carried out in this test, at four different angles, and on four different diagrams.

1 There was a greater tendency to mirror with the left hand than the right hand.

2 The amount of mirroring increased as the angle was increased.

3 The amount of mirroring varied with different diagrams and so also did the ratio of left- to right-hand mirroring.

4 A significantly greater percentage of boys than girls mirrored with the writing hand.

5 Inconsistency in the hand with which mirroring was performed as between different diagrams was shown by a considerable group of the subjects—184 out of 330.

6 Inconsistency in the hand with which mirroring was performed as between different angles on the same diagram was shown by an additional 43 subjects.

7 Of the total group of subjects, 123 out of 330 mirrored with neither hand or the non-writing hand first on each diagram. Of the remaining 207 subjects, 23 mirrored first with the writing hand. An analysis of their results on the other tests revealed little evidence of other left-hand tendencies in them.

8 Left-hand writers did, however, show a tendency to mirror with the right rather than the left hand, particularly in Figure 3.

9 An analysis of subjects giving inconsistent results indicated that no single diagram was causing the inconsistency.

10 A comparison between this test and the Simultaneous Writing Test showed that there was much more mirroring with the writing hand on the Van Riper Test, where the distraction was greater, and that there was no indication that those who mirrored with the writing hand on the one test tend to do so on the other.

11 A negative correlation was obtained between the total amount of mirroring produced with either hand and the intelligence of the subject, indicating that intelligence was influencing to some extent the angle at which mirroring would take place.

V THE WRITING TEST

1 No significant sex difference was found between the speed of writing of the right-handed boys and girls.

2 A low significant correlation was obtained between speed on the Writing Test where both speed and quality were emphasised and speed on the Speed of Crossing Test.

3 There was no apparent tendency for the left-hand writers

or those with left-hand tendencies to score below the mean of right-handers of the same sex.

4 The group of eighteen left-hand writers and of fourteen subjects with left-hand tendencies, when matched for sex, class and intelligence with right-handers, did not differ significantly in mean speed of writing from the paired right-handers.

5 Approximately equal numbers of the left-hand writers were judged better or worse than the paired right-handers, nine better, seven worse and two doubtful; while of those with left-hand tendencies, four were better than, and five worse than the paired right-handers—in the remaining five instances the observers were not agreed.

6 When both quality and speed were considered, four of the left-hand writers were better and quicker than the paired right-handers and three worse and slower; while one with left-hand tendencies was better and quicker than the paired right-hander and one worse and slower. Thus there was no tendency for the left-handers as a group to be poorer or slower than right-handers of the same sex, class and intelligence.

VI Results of the Left-Handers

1 The preference test results of the group of left-hand writers showed that they were not so uniform in their preference for the left hand as were many right-handers in their preference for the right hand.

2 There was a greater tendency towards left-eyedness among the left-hand writers than right-hand writers, only three out of eighteen left-hand writers were right-eyed on all tests of eyedness.

3 In the group with left-hand tendencies, all five subjects who had been changed to the right hand for writing were also right-eyed; while in contrast, the four subjects who still used the left hand in drawing and ruling lines were all left-eyed.

4 The Alternating Movement Test revealed a tendency in both groups of left-handers to be better with the left hand; while in the Fine Movement Test all the left-hand writers except two preferred the left hand, and five of those with left-hand tendencies preferred that hand.

5 A paired comparison of left-hand writers and right-hand

writers matched for sex, class and intelligence showed no significant difference between the mean Achievement Test result of the two groups.

6 The mean Achievement Test mark of the group of subjects with left-hand tendencies was significantly lower than that of right-handers with no such tendency when they were matched for sex, class and intelligence. The five subjects who had actually been changed to the right hand for writing were all more than twenty points below the paired right-handers in score on the Achievement Test.

VII SEX DIFFERENCE IN HANDEDNESS

1 A study of the writing hand of all the children attending the eight primary schools used in the present study gave the number of children writing with the left hand only as seven per cent (based on almost six thousand children aged between five and twelve years of age).

2 The percentage of left-hand writers was significantly higher among boys than among girls (8 and 5·9 per cent respectively).

3 In the total group of 330 subjects, 16 had left-handed fathers and 17 left-handed mothers, yet of 18 left-hand writers and 14 with strong left-hand tendencies 5 had a left-handed mother and none had a left-handed father.

CONCLUSIONS

1 Right-handedness is not a single factor existing in almost the entire human race with only one or two exceptions termed left-handed; nor can hand dominance be adequately described in terms of a dichotomous classification of right- and left-handedness appearing in unequal proportions. In short, differences in the proportion of right and left dominance are apparent not only in the total population, but also in the same person for different activities, the preponderance of right preference being greatest in those activities most connected with school writing. The number of persons showing consistent preference for one hand or the other appears also to vary for different activities and to be greatest in the more skilled and more often practised tasks. These results lead to the conclusion that no *single* test of hand dominance will give an adequate picture of handedness, and

that, though the results of different tests are positively correlated, a battery of tests is necessary for a study of even the more
important aspects.

2 Lateral asymmetry is a feature not only of use of the hand,
but also of foot, ear and eye. The presence of a connection
between the preference of foot and hand should be noted, and
the lack of connection between those of hand and eye. The
association found here, between the ear preferred in listening
and the preferred eye, when the subjects were unaware that
either of these aspects was being tested, is also worth noting.
However, since visual and aural acuity were not tested, it may
be that, in the subjects showing such a connection, acuity was
in some way involved, an aspect which may warrant further
investigation.

3 The inclusion of the Van Riper Critical Angle Board as a
diagnostic instrument for measuring left-handedness has not
been justified by the findings of this study because of the inconsistency of the results on different diagrams and at different
angles, and by the connection of the total mirroring with
intelligence. Since no reliability can be placed on the critical
angle as a measure of degree of dominance, it would seem that
future research might profitably be confined to the 90 degree
or 'back to back' position of the boards where mirroring most
often occurs.

4 Writing difficulties of left-handers and the analysis of their
writing as compared with that of right-handers is a subject of
some practical importance. The absence of a significant difference between the speed or quality of writing of the left-handers
and right-handers in this study reveals only the probable
absence of a general connection. Though indicating that left-
hand writers are not inevitably slower or poorer than right-hand
writers as a result only of using the left hand, the conclusion
should not be drawn that there are no left-handers whose
writing is suffering either in speed or in quality. Some valuable
information might be secured by an investigation of the relative
scores of a larger number of older left- and right-handers on
such single aspects as speed, legibility, quality, pressure, and,
possibly most important of all, fatigue from long periods of
writing.

5 Left-hand writers, as this study has shown, represent only a fraction of those with left-hand tendencies. Some have been changed to the right hand, others have transferred of their own volition after commencing writing lessons, while still others have been changed even before entering school. The percentage of children using the left hand for writing seems to be increasing; a more extensive survey of the present incidence in different districts and among different age groups is, however, required.

6 It is not desired to over-stress the findings obtained in the present study on the achievement scores because the number of pupils is limited and the achievement tests were not personally administered. They do seem, nevertheless, to suggest a most important line for future research, namely, to establish the truth of the indication that, though left-hand writers are not poorer in scholastic achievement than right-handers, right-hand writers with left-hand tendencies may be poorer in scholastic attainment. If this were proved, it would have a significant bearing on the vexed problem of whether or not any attempt should be made to get a left-handed child to use his right hand.

In conclusion it is worth pointing out that no essential difference was apparent between left-handers and right-handers, except for their use of a different hand. This is no empty statement; on the contrary, it is a finding which requires to be emphasised in view of current attitudes to the phenomenon of left-handedness. It is imperative that the same attention be given to teaching left-handers to write with the left hand as is devoted to right-handers. Unsuspected instances of left-handedness, or left-handers changed to right-handedness, may suffer from enforced use of the non-dominant hand; means should accordingly be found to ascertain such cases and make provision for them. Further research should be undertaken to devise reliable instruments for the measurement of handedness and to produce more satisfactory scales of measurement.

APPENDIX

INCIDENCE OF LEFT-HANDEDNESS IN A 10-11-YEAR-OLD AGE-GROUP OF SCOTTISH CHILDREN

	BOYS			GIRLS			TOTAL		
	Number Left-handed	Number observed	Per cent	Number Left-handed	Number observed	Per cent	Number Left-handed	Number observed	Per cent
Cities - - - -	991	12629	7·84	487	12416	3·91	1478	25045	5·89
Mainly industrial areas -	427	7651	5·58	310	7660	4·04	737	15311	4·81
Mixed industrial and rural areas -	469	7904	5·93	364	7649	4·75	833	15553	5·35
Mainly rural areas - -	364	5378	5·69	268	5161	5·19	632	10539	5·99
Mainly heath and moor -	101	1912	5·28	83	1947	4·26	184	3859	4·76
Private schools - -	82	953	8·60	70	978	7·15	152	1931	7·87
All - - -	2434	36427	6·68	1582	35811	4·41	4016	72238	5·5

These figures were obtained in the 1953 Scholastic Survey of a complete age-group of Scottish children (approximately 10-11 years). The teacher observed whether the pupil wrote the tests with the left or right hand.

BIBLIOGRAPHY

AMES, L B, 'Supine Leg and Foot Postures in the Human Infant in the First Year of Life', *Journal of Genetic Psychology*, vol LXI, 1942, pp 87-107

BILLINGS, M L, 'A Report of a Case of Inverted Writing and Drawing', *Child Development*, vol VI, No 2, 1935, pp 161-163

BLAU, A, *The Master Hand*, New York: The American Orthopsychiatric Association, 1946

BLOM, E C, 'Mirror-Writing', *Psychological Bulletin*, vol XXV, 1928, pp 582-592

BRAIN, R, 'Speech and Handedness', *Lancet*, vol CCXLIX, No 2, 1945, pp 837-841

BROCK, S, *The Basis of Clinical Neurology*, Baltimore: Williams and Wilkins Co, 1937

BRYNGELSON, B, 'Stuttering and Personality Development', *Nervous Child*, vol II, No 2, 1942, pp 162-166

—— and T B CLARK, 'Left-handedness and Stuttering', *Journal of Heredity*, vol XXIV, 1933, pp 387-390

BUCHANAN, A, 'Mechanical Theory of the Predominance of the Right Hand over the Left', *Proceedings of the Philosophical Society of Glasgow*, vol V, 1862, pp 142-167

—— 'On the Position of the Centre of Gravity in Man, as Determining the Mechanical Relations of the Two Sides of the Body Towards Each Other', *Proceedings of the Philosophical Society of Glasgow*, vol X, No 2, 1877, pp 390-413

BURT, C, *The Backward Child*, London: University of London Press, 1937

BUXTON, C E and H R CROSLAND, 'The Concept of Eye-Preference', *American Journal of Psychology*, vol XLIX, 1937, pp 458-461

CARMICHAEL, L, (Ed), *Manual of Child Psychology*, New York: John Wiley and Sons, Inc, 1946

CASTNER, B M, 'The Incidence of Sinistral Types among Children Referred to a Psychological Clinic', *Psychological Bulletin*, vol XXX, 1933, p 727

CHAMBERLAIN, H D, 'The Inheritance of Left-handedness', *Journal of Heredity*, vol XIX, 1928, pp 557-559

CHANDLER, C M, 'Hand, Eye and Foot Preferences of Two Hundred Psychotic Patients and Two Hundred Students', *Psychological Bulletin*, vol XXXI, 1934, pp 593-594

CHESHER, E C, 'Some Observations Concerning the Relation of Handedness to the Language Mechanism', *Bulletin of the Neurological Institute of New York*, No IV, 1936, pp 556-562

CHRYSANTHIS, K, 'Stammering and Handedness', *Lancet*, vol CCLII, 1947, pp 270-271

COLE, L, *Psychology of the Elementary School Subjects*, New York: Farrar and Rinehart, Inc, 1934

—— 'Instruction in Penmanship for the Left-Handed Child', *Elementary School Journal*, vol XXXIX, 1939, pp 436-448

CRIDER, B, 'Unilateral Sighting Preference', *Child Development*, vol VI, No 2, 1935, pp 163-164

—— 'The Relationship of Eye Muscle Balance to the Sighting Eye', *Journal of Experimental Psychology*, vol XVIII, 1935, pp 152-154

CUFF, N B, 'The Interpretation of Handedness', *Journal of Experimental Psychology*, vol XI, 1928, pp 27-39

—— 'A Study of Eyedness and Handedness', *Journal of Experimental Psychology*, vol XIV, 1931, pp 164-175

DART, C, 'The Hand, Eye and Foot Preference of Two Hundred Mentally Subnormal Subjects and Two Hundred Subjects of Normal or Superior Intelligence', *Psychological Bulletin*, vol XXXI, 1934, p 593

DARWIN, C, 'A Biographical Sketch of an Infant', *Mind*, vol II, 1877, pp 285-294

DEARBORN, W F, 'Ocular and Manual Dominance in Dyslexia', *Psychological Bulletin*, vol XXVIII, 1931, p 704

DENNIS, W, 'Laterality of Function in Early Infancy under Controlled Developmental Conditions', *Child Development*, vol VI, 1935, pp 242-252

DOWNEY, J E, 'Back-Slanted Writing and Sinistral Tendencies', *Journal of Educational Psychology*, vol XXIII, 1932, pp 277-286

—— 'Laterality of Function', *Psychological Bulletin*, vol XXX, 1933, pp 109-142

EYRE, M B, and M M SCHMECKLE, 'A Study of Handedness, Eyedness and Footedness', *Child Development*, vol IV, 1933, pp 73-78

FERNALD, G R, *Remedial Work in the Basic Skill Subjects*, New York: The McGraw-Hill Book Co, 1943

FREEMAN, F N, *Solving Handwriting Needs As We See Them Today*, Columbus, Ohio: Zaner-Bloser Co, nd

FULLER, J K, 'The Psychology and Physiology of Mirror-Writing', *University of California Publications in Psychology*, vol II, No 3, 1916, pp 199-265

GAHAGAN, L, 'Visual Dominance-Acuity Relationships', *Journal of General Psychology*, vol IX, 1933, pp 455-459

GARDNER, W H, *Left Handed Writing—Instruction Manual*, Danville, Ill: The Interstate Co, 1945

GATES, A I, *The Improvement of Reading*, New York: The Macmillan Co, 1937

—— and G L BOND, 'Relation of Handedness, Eye-Sighting and Acuity Dominance to Reading', *Journal of Educational Psychology*, vol XXVII, 1936, pp 450-456

GESELL, A, et al, *The First Five Years of Life—A Guide to the Study of the Preschool Child*, London: Methuen and Co, Ltd, nd

—— and L B Ames, 'The Development of Handedness', *Journal of Genetic Psychology*, vol LXX, 1947, pp 155-175

GORDON, H, 'Left-Handedness and Mirror-Writing, Especially among Defective Children', *Brain*, vol XLIII, 1921, pp 313-368

GOULD, G M, *Righthandedness and Lefthandedness*, Philadelphia: J B Lippincott Co, 1908

HAEFNER, R, *Educational Significance of Left-Handedness*, Contributions to Education No 360, New York: Bureau of Publications, Teachers College, Columbia University, 1929

HALL, G S, 'Notes on the Study of Infants', *Pedagogical Seminary*, vol I, 1891, pp 127-138

HARRIS, A J, *Harris Tests of Lateral Dominance*: Manual of Directions for Administration and Interpretation, New York: The Psychological Corporation, 1947

HERREN, R Y, and D B LINDSLEY, 'A Note Concerning Cerebral Dominance in the Rat', *Journal of Genetic Psychology*, vol XLVII, 1935, pp 469-472

HILDRETH, G, 'Bilateral Manual Performance, Eye-Dominance and Reading Achievement', *Child Development*, vol XI, No 4, 1940, pp 311-317

—— 'A School Survey of Eye-Hand Dominance', *Journal of Applied Psychology*, vol XXIX, 1945, pp 83-88

—— 'Manual Dominance in Nursery School Children', *Journal of Genetic Psychology*, vol LXXII, 1948, pp 29-45

—— 'Development and Training of Hand Dominance: IV Developmental Problems Associated with Handedness, V Training of Handedness', *Journal of Genetic Psychology*, vol LXXVI, 1950, pp 39-144

HULL, C J, 'A Study of Laterality Test Items', *Journal of Experimental Education*, vol IV, No 3, 1936, pp 287-290

HUMPHREY, M E, 'Consistency of Hand Usage', *British Journal of Educational Psychology*, vol XXI, 1951, pp 214-225

HUMPHRY, G M, *The Human Foot and the Human Hand*, Cambridge, England: The Macmillan Co, 1861

INMAN, W S, 'Inquiry into the Origin of Squint, Left-Handedness and Stammer', *Lancet*, vol CCVII, No II, 1924, pp 211-215

JACKSON, J, *Ambidexterity*, London: Kegan Paul and Co, Ltd, 1905

JASPER, H H, 'A Laboratory Study of Diagnostic Indices of Bilateral Neuromuscular Organisation in Stutterers and Normal Speakers', *Psychological Monographs*, vol XLIII, No 1, 1932, pp 72-174

—— and E T RANEY, 'The Phi Test of Lateral Dominance', *American Journal of Psychology*, vol XLIX, 1937, pp 450-457

—— —— 'The Physiology of Lateral Cerebral Dominance', *Psychological Bulletin*, vol XXXIV, 1937, pp 151-165

JOHNSON, W, 'The Dominant Thumb in Relation to Stuttering,

Eyedness and Handedness', *American Journal of Psychology*, vol XLIX, 1937, pp 293-297

—— and L DUKE, 'Change of Handedness Associated with the Onset or Disappearance of Stuttering: Sixteen Cases', *Journal of Experimental Education*, vol IV, No 2, 1935, pp 112-132

—— and D DUKE, 'The Dextrality Quotients of Fifty Six-year-olds with Regard to Hand Usage', *Journal of Educational Psychology*, vol XXVII, 1936, pp 26-36

—— and A KING, 'An Angle Board and Hand Usage Study of Stutterers and Non-Stutterers', *Journal of Experimental Psychology*, vol XXXI, 1942, pp 293-311

JORDAN, H E, 'Hereditary Left-Handedness with a Note on Twinning', *Journal of Genetics*, vol IV, 1914, pp 67-81

KELLY, G A, 'Some Observations on the Relation of the Principle of Physiological Polarity and Symmetry and the Doctrine of Cerebral Dominance to the Perception of Symbols', *Journal of Experimental Psychology*, vol XVIII, 1935, pp 202-213

KLEIN, R, 'Dynamic Factors in Aphasia', *Journal of Mental Science*, vol XCV, 1949, pp 874-879

KOPP, H, 'The Relationship of Stuttering to Motor Disturbances', *Nervous Child*, vol II, No 2, 1942, pp 107-116

LAUTERBACH, C E, 'Studies in Twin Resemblance', *Genetics*, vol X, 1925, pp 525-568

LEHMAN, H C, and F E WEBB, 'Left-Handedness among Major League Baseball Players', *Motor Skills Research Exchange*, vol III, No 1, University of Louisville, 1951

LUND, F H, 'The Dependence of Eye-Hand Co-ordination upon Eye-Dominance', *American Journal of Psychology*, vol XLIV, 1932, pp 756-762

—— 'The Monoptometer: A New Device for Measuring Eye-Dominance', *American Journal of Psychology*, vol XLIV, 1932, pp 181-183

MCALLISTER, A H, *Clinical Studies in Speech Therapy*, London: University of London Press, 1937

MACMEEKEN, A M, *Ocular Dominance in Relation to Developmental Aphasia*, London: University of London Press, Ltd, 1939

—— *Developmental Aphasia in Educationally Retarded Children*, London: University of London Press, Ltd, 1942

MILES, W R, 'Ocular Dominance, Demonstrated by Unconscious Sighting', *Journal of Experimental Psychology*, vol XII, 1929, pp 113-126

MILESEN, R, 'The Effect of Training upon the Handedness Preference of the Rat in an Eating Activity', *Psychological Monographs*, vol XLIX, No 1, 1937, pp 234-243

MINTZ, A, 'A Study of Indications of Unstable Unilateral Cerebral Dominance, Reading Disability, and Mental Deficiency,' *Psychological Bulletin*, vol XXX, 1933, pp 565-566

MINTZ, A, 'Reading Reversals and Lateral Preferences in a Group of Intellectually Subnormal Boys', *Journal of Educational Psychology*, vol XXXVII, 1946, pp 487-501

MONROE, M, *Children Who Cannot Read*, Chicago: University of Chicago Press, 1932

NEWMAN, H H, F N FREEMAN and K J HOLZINGER, *Twins: A Study of Heredity and Environment*, Chicago: The University of Chicago Press, 1937, pp 12, 39-48

NIELSON, J M, *A Textbook of Clinical Neurology*, New York: Paul B Hoeber Inc, 1946

OJEMANN, R H, 'Studies in Handedness: IA-Technique for Testing Unimanual Handedness', *Journal of Educational Psychology*, vol XXI, 1930, pp 597-611

ORTON, S T, *Reading, Writing and Speech Problems in Children*, London: Chapman and Hall Ltd, 1937

PARSON, B S, *Lefthandedness—A New Interpretation*, New York: The Macmillan Co, 1924

PETERSON, G M, 'A Preliminary Report on Right-and Left-Handedness in the Rat', *Journal of Comparative Psychology*, vol XII, 1931, pp 243-250

—— 'The Influence of Cerebral Destructions upon the Handedness of the Rat in the Latch Box', *Journal of Comparative Psychology*, vol XXVI, 1938, pp 445-457

—— 'Changes in Handedness in the Rat by Local Application of Acetylcholine to the Cerebral Cortex', *Journal of Comparative and Physiological Psychology*, vol XLII, 1949, pp 404-413

PHELPS, W M, and T A TURNER, 'Left Hand, Right Hand', *Hygeia*, November 1948, pp 808-809, 822

PYE-SMITH, P H, 'On Left-Handedness', *Guy's Hospital Reports*, Third Series, vol XVI, 1871, pp 141-146

RAMALEY, F, 'Inheritance of Left-Handedness', *American Naturalist*, vol XLVII, 1913, p 564

RHEINBERGER, M B, I W KARLIN and A B BERMAN, 'Electroencephalographic and Laterality Studies of Stuttering and Non-Stuttering Children', *Nervous Child*, vol II, No 2, 1942, pp 117-133

RIFE, J M, 'Types of Dextrality', *Psychological Review*, vol XXIX, 1922, pp 474-480

RIFE, D C, 'Genetic Studies of Monozygotic Twins, Part III, Mirror-Imaging', *Journal of Heredity*, vol XXIV, 1933, pp 443-446

—— 'Handedness with Special Reference to Twins', *Genetics*, vol XXV, 1940, pp 178-186

ROBERTS, W W, 'The Interpretation of Some Disorders of Speech', *Journal of Mental Science*, vol XCV, 1949, pp 567-588

ROOS, M M, 'A Study of Some Factors entering into the Determination of Handedness', *Child Development*, vol VI, No 2, 1935, pp 91-97

P

Roos, M M, 'Variations with Age in Frequency Distribution of Degrees of Handedness', *Child Development*, vol VI, No 4, 1935, pp 259-268

Rusk, R R, 'An Illustration of Synthesis in Research', *Educational Research*, Supplement to the *Head Teachers' Review*, vol VII, No 3, 1929

Scheidemann, N V and G E Robinette, 'Testing the Ocular Dominance of Infants', *Psychological Clinic*, vol XXI, 1932, pp 62-63

Schoen, Z J and C F Scofield, 'A Study of the Relative Neuromuscular Efficiency of the Dominant and Non-Dominant Eye in Binocular Vision', *Journal of General Psychology*, vol XII, 1935, pp 156-181

Schonell, F J, *Backwardness in the Basic Subjects*, London: Oliver and Boyd, 1942, pp 162-169

Smith, G Elliot, *The Evolution of Man*, Oxford: Oxford University Press, 1924, pp 42-43

—— 'Right- and Left-Handedness in Primitive Men', *British Medical Journal*, vol II, 1925, pp 1107-1108

Smith, L C, 'A Study of Laterality Characteristics of Retarded Readers and Reading Achievers', *Journal of Experimental Education*, vol XVIII, No 4, 1950, pp 321-329 (the thesis of which that is a summary, submitted in 1949 for the degree of Doctor of Education to Teachers' College, Temple University, was also consulted)

Spache, G, 'A Binocular Reading Test', *Journal of Applied Psychology*, vol XXVII, 1943, pp 109-113

Scottish Council for Research in Education, *Studies in Reading*, vol I, London: University of London Press Ltd, 1948, pp 29-42

Staff of the Reading Clinics of the University of Chicago, *Clinical Studies in Reading I*, Supplementary Educational Monographs, No 68, Chicago: University of Chicago Press, 1949

Trankell, A, *Vänsterhänthet hos Barn i Skolaldern*, Helsinfors: Mercators Tryckeri, 1950 (contains a summary in English)

Travis, L E, 'A Comparative Study of the Performance of Stutterers and Normal Speakers in Mirror Tracing', *Psychological Monographs*, vol XXXIX, 1928, pp 45-50

—— *Speech Pathology*, New York: D Appleton-Century Co, 1931

—— and W Johnson, 'Stuttering and the Concept of Handedness', *Psychological Review*, vol XLI, 1934, pp 534-562

Tsai, L S and S Maurer, 'Right-Handedness in White Rats', *Science*, vol LXXII, 1930, pp 436-438

Updegraff, R, 'Preferential Handedness in Young Children', *Journal of Experimental Education*, 1932, pp 134-139

—— 'The Correspondence between Handedness and Eyedness in Young Children', *Pedagogical Seminary*, vol XLII, 1933, pp 490-492

Van Riper, C, 'A New Test of Laterality', *Journal of Experimental Psychology*, vol XVII, 1934, pp 305-313

VAN RIPER, C, 'The Quantitative Measurement of Laterality', *Journal of Experimental Psychology*, vol XVIII, 1935, pp 372-382

—— *Speech Correction, Principles and Methods*, New York: Prentice-Hall, Inc, 1947

WALLS, G L, 'A Theory of Ocular Dominance', A M A, *Archives of Ophthalmology*, vol XLV, No 4, 1951, pp 387-412

WARREN, N, and B CLARK, 'A Consideration of the Use of the Term Ocular Dominance', *Psychological Bulletin*, vol XXXV, 1938, pp 298-304

WASHBURN, M F, C FAISON and R SCOTT, 'A Comparison Between the Miles A-B-C Method and Retinal Rivalry as Tests of Ocular Dominance', *American Journal of Psychology*, vol XLVI, 1934, pp 633-636

WEST, P V, *Changing Practice in Handwriting Instruction*, Blooming-ton, Ill: Public School Publishing Co, 1927, pp 55-56

—— Manual for the American Handwriting Scale, New York: The A N Palmer Co, 1929

WEST, R, 'The Pathology of Stuttering', *Nervous Child*, vol II, No 2, 1942, pp 97-106

WHIPPLE, G M, *Manual of Mental and Physical Tests* Part I, Balti-more: Warwick and York Inc, 1914

WHITE, A M, and K M DALLENBACH, 'Position versus Intensity as a Determinant of the Attention of Left-Handed Observers', *American Journal of Psychology*, vol XLIV, 1932, pp 175-178

WILE, I S, *Handedness: Right and Left*, Boston: Lothrop Lee and Shepard, 1934

WILSON, D, *The Right Hand: Left-Handedness*, London: Nature Series, The Macmillan Co, 1891

WILSON, P T, and H E JONES, 'Left-Handedness in Twins', *Genetics*, vol XVII, 1932, pp 560-571

WITTENBORN, J R, 'Correlates of Handedness among College Fresh-men', *Journal of Educational Psychology*, vol XXXVII, 1946, pp 161-170

WITTY, P A, and D KOPEL, 'Sinistral and Mixed Manual-Ocular Behaviour in Reading Disability', *Journal of Educational Psycho-logy*, vol XXVII, 1936, pp 119-134

WOLFE, L S, 'An Experimental Study of Reversals in Reading', *American Journal of Psychology*, vol LII, 1939, pp 533-561

WOO, T L, and K PEARSON, 'Dextrality and Sinistrality of Hand and Eye', *Biometrika*, vol XIX, 1927, pp 165-199

WOODY, C, and A J PHILLIPS, 'The Effects of Handedness on Rever-sals in Reading', *Journal of Educational Research*, vol XXVII, 1934, pp 651, 662

WOOLLEY, H T, 'The Development of Right-Handedness in a Normal Infant', *Psychological Review*, vol XVII, 1910, pp 34-41

YERKES, R M, *Chimpanzees, A Laboratory Colony*, pp 113-115, New Haven: Yale University Press, 1943

INDEX OF NAMES

INDEX OF TOPICS AND TITLES

PUBLICATIONS OF THE
SCOTTISH COUNCIL FOR RESEARCH IN EDUCATION

I SCOTTISH SPINNING SCHOOLS (With illustrations)
By IRENE F M DEAN, FRHistSoc 5/- net

II EDUCATION IN ANGUS
By J C JESSOP, MA, PhD, FRHistSoc 5/- net

III CURRICULUM FOR PUPILS OF TWELVE TO FIFTEEN
YEARS (Advanced Division) (out of print)
Subject Reports available, each 6d net

IV GROUP TEST FOR COLOUR BLINDNESS (out of print)
By MARY COLLINS, MA, BEd, PhD, and JAMES DREVER, MA, BSc,
DPhil, and lithographed by C C PARKINSON 10/6 net

V THE INTELLIGENCE OF SCOTTISH CHILDREN
5/- net

VI ACHIEVEMENT TESTS IN THE PRIMARY SCHOOL
By GREGOR MACGREGOR, MA, BSc, FEIS (out of print)

VII A HISTORY OF SCOTTISH EXPERIMENTS IN RURAL
EDUCATION
By JOHN MASON, MA, PhD 5/- net

VIII THE HISTORY OF MATHEMATICAL TEACHING IN
SCOTLAND
By DUNCAN K WILSON, MA, BSc, PhD (out of print) 5/- net

IX THE PROGNOSTIC VALUE OF UNIVERSITY ENTRANCE
EXAMINATIONS IN SCOTLAND
5/- net

X TESTS OF ABILITY FOR SECONDARY SCHOOL
COURSES
By FRANK M EARLE, MEd, DSc (out of print) 5/- net

XI CITY AND RURAL SCHOOLS (out of print)
By ALEX S MOWAT, MA, BEd 1/- net

XII THE STANDARDISATION OF A GRADED WORD
READING TEST
By P E VERNON, MA, PhD 1/- net
Test cards reprinted from the above:
1 THE GRADED WORD READING TEST 4d plus 1d purchase tax per copy
2 THE BURT (Rearranged) WORD READING TEST
4d plus 1d purchase tax per copy

XIII STUDIES IN ARITHMETIC, Volume I (out of print)
5/- net

XIV SCOTTISH PRIMARY SCHOOL ORGANISATION
1/- net

XV THE INTELLIGENCE OF A REPRESENTATIVE GROUP
OF SCOTTISH CHILDREN (out of print)
By A M MacMEEKEN, MA, BEd, Phd 5/- net

XVI AN ANALYSIS OF PERFORMANCE TEST SCORES OF A
REPRESENTATIVE GROUP OF SCOTTISH CHILDREN
By SIR GODFREY THOMSON, PhD, DSc, DCL, FEIS(Hon) 5/- net

XVII THE ASSESSMENT OF EDUCATIONAL FILMS
(out of print) 1/- net

XVIII STUDIES IN ARITHMETIC, Volume II (out of print)
5/- net

XIX SELECTION FOR SECONDARY EDUCATION
By WILLIAM McCLELLAND, CBE, MA, BSc, BEd, FRSE, FEIS 5/- net

XX THE EARLY DEVELOPMENT OF NUMBER CONCEPTS
(out of print) 1/- net

XXI THE TEACHING OF ARITHMETIC
By JOHN MORRISON, MBE, MA, BSc 1/- net

213

THE SCOTTISH PUPIL'S SPELLING BOOK
Parts I and II   1/2 each
Parts III, IV and V 1/- each
Teacher's Book   8/6